They Ride White Horses

They Ride White Horses

The End of the Search for Significance

David Graham

They Ride White Horses
— *The End of the Search for Significance*

Published by PCG Legacy,
a division of Pilot Communications Group, Inc.
317 Appaloosa Trail
Waco TX 76712

ISBN: 9781936417261

Printed in the United States of America

Contact the author:
www.theyridewhitehorses.com

Dedication

To Kathy — my dear wife, best friend, and one of the most wonderful caregivers I've ever known. She's always been there by my side, even when my side wanted to go sideways.

And to my children Michelle, Kimberly, Jeffrey, and Michael, who, more than anyone else, helped me to "see" and understand just how much the Father in heaven loves us all.

Acknowledgments

I'm so grateful to all my family and friends, who encouraged me to write and then gave of their time along the way.

Special thanks to Claire Hughes, who generously reworked a good part of the first manuscript — just before I put it on the shelf for fourteen years. I'm most indebted to my dear friend, Bob Daniels, who almost forced me to take the dusty manuscript *off* the shelf, labored with me to create a new, more complete version, and then *gently* hounded me, as he says, like a sheepdog, to get the project and me into the corral.

Much love and thanks to my son-in-law, Jason, and to my daughter, Kimberly, for their further editing and insight. Thanks as well to Donna Briggs of Mission Builders International for her unceasing encouragement, to Brenda Mallaburn (Brenda Mallaburn Photography and Graphic Design) and Damien Mayfield for their collaborative help in bringing the cover to life, and to my friend and publisher, Brian Mast, at PCG Legacy, for putting all the pieces together.

And finally, a standing ovation to our wonderful friend and final editor, Becky Hefty, who put her "all" into making sure the message of the book could finally be read. I affectionately call her Mrs. Bunyan because she carries a big axe when it comes to words and phrases that aren't *just right*. Thank you, Becky.

Contents

Foreword

My father is an extraordinary man. As a child, when my dad walked through the door at the end of each day, my world became perfect. When he was there, I knew everything would be all right. When he spoke to me, they were words of comfort and wisdom. If I had a question, I knew he had the answer. The man who was my dad was one of strength and decisiveness, impervious to any weakness. That was the only dad I knew.

I was oblivious to his personal struggle, to the battle waged inside of him as he wrestled with his identity, self-esteem, and insecurities. I was unaware of the fear that crept up on him and the attacks he faced in his days. What an incredible gift to have parents who can be who they need to be for their children; who rise to the challenge to nurture and love in spite of experiencing pain. My father's arms felt strong, his words seemed assured. The little girl only saw the hero, the warrior, but never knew until adulthood how determinedly her dad fought to overcome.

The journey my dad has traveled is detailed in this book. Through his brokenness and weakness came revelation and understanding of God as his Father in a most incredible way. Throughout these chapters, my dad encounters the Spirit. The Spirit counsels and teaches him about a simple truth, which, like so many other people, he was missing. His view of God became intimate, and what he learned would be the key to combating the immobilizing fear and insecurity that had plagued him.

I was a fortunate child to have had a father who made me feel precious. Greater still was the influence my dad's revelation had on my life as I grew to believe I was even more precious in my heavenly Father's eyes. What a gift I was given. What a gift available to all!

As you read this book, know how precious and significant you are as a daughter, as a son of your heavenly Father who is, as my dad says, "the ultimate parent." My prayer is that Dad's testimony will inspire you to grab hold of God's immeasurable love for you and to claim that which is yours: an abundant inheritance.

— *Kimberly Graham Bridwell*

Introduction

From my earliest years I heard and believed that God loved us and had the answers to all of life's situations. Over the years, as a Christian leader and teacher, I spoke out those beliefs hundreds of times to hundreds of people until the day — in spite of all my faith, knowledge, and experience — I suffered a sudden emotional crash. In a matter of moments, the most horrible of my life, I was thrust into an arduous journey down a path of fear and introspection. It was here I came face to face with another part of myself — an insecure self, that part of me battling for a sense of significance, well-being, and purpose.

It's accepted that the majority of human beings struggle, at least to some degree, with these same issues. The problem is most often traced to childhood when parents, who had the same problem, couldn't or didn't give their child sufficient validation and security. Though it may only live in the subconscious, many of us feel hurt, even damaged, by those we expected would take perfect care of us. For some of us, it was a small hurt. For some of us, it was big. Whatever the case, the result is things aren't the way they should be. *Things aren't the way they can be.*

The world isn't short on suggested remedies for fixing injured lives: striving to achieve, trying the "self-help" approach, being "religious" — just to name a few. We pursue such antidotes in an effort to feel more whole. But what grabbed hold of me in my frustrating state of weakness was a powerful truth — a truth so central to the heart of the New Testament, yet I'd never "seen" it before. It was so simple and yet so profound. It rocked me to the core when I finally "got it."

Since that time, I have shared my story before thousands of people. Many of them have come up to me with tears in their eyes, and asked, "Why haven't I seen this before?"

As you read my story, I believe there is a real possibility God will show *you* something *you've* never seen before — something new, yet as old as Eden.

— *David Graham*

PART ONE

What Is Going On Here?

I have dealt with only three fears in my life:
fear of man, fear of failure, and fear of death.
Otherwise, I've been just great.

Chapter 1

A Victim of Fear

*My thoughts trouble me and I am distraught.… My heart is
in anguish within me; the terrors of death assail me. Fear and
trembling have beset me; horror has overwhelmed me.*
— Psalm 55:2-4

———

*T*he wheels hit the runway with a screech at Spokane
International Airport in Spokane, Washington, and the 737
roared down into taxi speed. It was late winter of 1982, and I
was trying to get home from a business trip to Dallas, Texas. Before the
plane had even come to a stop, I was out of my seat; leaving my coat,
garment bag, and briefcase behind. In desperation, I shoved my way
toward the front exit. As the head flight attendant began opening the
door, I joined her, much to her surprise and annoyance. I lunged
forward like a crazed man, gasping for breath with each step, until I
could make myself move no farther. I leaned hard against the jet-way
wall, staring down the blurred walkway, then slumped into a human
ball on the floor.

In an instant, two flight attendants were helping me to my feet. I leaned on them for support as they escorted me through the gateway and into a private room. Hobbling into the room, shaking from head to foot, I promptly collapsed. One of the attendants gently stroked my head. "Everything is going to be alright," she said. I didn't believe her. Not long after, two men in white coats lifted me onto a rollaway stretcher and wheeled me through the crowded airport. Within minutes, I was in an ambulance and on my way to a Spokane hospital.

———

Three-and-a-half years earlier, I had decided to take an extended leave of absence from full-time ministry after a series of events led me to question "the call" I had felt so strongly since I was twenty-two years of age. By a seeming stroke of the miraculous, I found a position as sales manager for a local manufacturing company, a role that required a lot of travel. Though I felt somewhat confident about the public relations side of things, I was wary from the outset about my ability to get a firm handle on product and industry knowledge. As time went by, the products I sold became more sophisticated; my wariness became anxiety.

Each trip took an increasing toll on me. It was on a Friday morning, my final day in Dallas, things really heated up. On my way up a flight of stairs to meet with a company executive, I suddenly felt light-headed and dizzy. Something wasn't right. It was hard to breath; my chest felt tight. In the hallway at the top of the stairs, I stopped and sagged against the wall in an effort to regain control.

While recovering from the mysterious episode, I noticed to my left a robotic cart moving down the hall in my direction carrying mail and memos for delivery to different offices. Studying the non-human as it rolled by, I was almost certain it shot me a suspicious, perhaps even smug glance as it rounded the corner and passed from my sight. It was an odd and troubling experience.

Speechless and still catching my breath, I found myself asking: *Just what is the meaning of life, anyway? What is my significance? What am I doing here?*

I proceeded without enthusiasm to make my last call of the week. The executive in charge wasn't interested in my product, and at that point, I really didn't care. All I wanted was to get out of there and go home to my family.

———

Dallas Fort Worth Airport was packed with Friday business travelers. All the lines to the ticket counters were close to a hundred people deep, and they weren't moving fast. Fearing I wouldn't make my flight, I felt the tension rise in me. It took almost an hour to get to the counter where a very gruff ticket agent informed me there would be a delay due to mechanical difficulties. *"That's just great,"* I complained, half out loud. Grabbing my stuff, I made my way to the gate area.

After two more frustrating hours, I went to the gate agent to ask what the status was. His answer bordered on rude. Verbal confrontation had never been in my nature, but this turned into one. When I finished spewing out a few heated words, I walked away, quaking on the inside and uncharacteristically angry. I shook for most of the next hour until we boarded at last, hours behind schedule.

When the plane finally landed in Seattle, my connecting flight to Spokane was still on the ground; but of course, its gate was the very last one on the far side of the terminal. Racing down the concourse like a madman, I arrived at the airplane door just as it was about to swing shut. I shouted desperately, and an attendant opened the door, allowing me to board.

Shuffling down the aisle to my seat, I flopped down, expecting a sense of relief to comfort me. But to my horror, before I could even put on my seatbelt, I was suddenly drenched in cold sweat, my heart racing. Waves of nausea engulfed me. I started trembling and my neck went rigid. As the plane roared down the runway for takeoff, I began to hyperventilate and leaned my head against the seat in front of me, weeping. A baseless terror gripped me in a way I had never even imagined possible. The man seated next to me bent forward and asked, "Are you okay?"

"I don't know," I whispered. I hated that he was concerned. His question only intensified my fear — I was coming apart and couldn't hide it.

Hemmed in by seats, people, and the shrinking plane compartment, my anxiety mounted with each passing second. All I could think about was how to get off my "flight from hell." So intense was my panic, I considered *begging* the attendant to make the captain turn the plane around. The moments seemed like millennia. Yet as frightening as the whole experience had been up to this point, it was only a taste of what was to come.

———

While the ambulance tore down the highway toward downtown Spokane, the paramedic radioed my blood pressure and other vitals to the hospital. Nothing seemed real. *This couldn't be happening to me,* I thought.

In no time I was out of the ambulance and under the bright lights of the hospital emergency room, surrounded by six or eight medical professionals. They asked questions while hooking me up to various machines, then, one by one, backed away and huddled in a circle on the far side of the room. After several minutes, the doctor in charge stood beside me.

"Mr. Graham?"

"Yes," I replied feebly. "What's wrong with me, Doctor?"

"You're not having a heart attack, which was our first concern. You're having a panic attack."

"A panic attack? What's a panic attack?"

"It's what you're having," he said, as if that somehow answered my question. If he'd said heart attack, I would have understood. A heart you can maybe fix. But how do you fix panic?

"Well, what do we do, Doctor, what do we *do*?"

"First of all, Mr. Graham, I'm going to give you a shot to relax you. I'm also going to give you a bottle of Valium, a kind of tranquilizer. I want you to try and get a good night's sleep in a nearby hotel — and you probably need to see a counselor."

What? I thought indignantly. *A counselor? I am a counselor!*

The hospital staff called a taxi for me, and I was soon at a hotel where I did *not* get a good night's sleep. Although still under sedation, I was thoroughly baffled by the emotions and physical effects of my "hell day." As I paced the tiny hotel room for hours, the fear quieted, but it didn't leave.

The next morning I decided that facing a forty-five minute flight from Spokane to my hometown in Montana was impossible — I wasn't taking any more chances with flight delays or enclosed spaces. Instead, I rented a car and began the five-hour, mountainous drive home. Two-thirds of the way there, on the lonely, winding stretch of Montana highway that crosses the Flathead Indian Reservation from Plains to Elmo, it hit me again. Pulling over, I got out and began walking around the car in circles, kicking the tires on each pass. I didn't think I could go on. I leaned up against a front fender, shaking and crying, as a light snow began falling on the silent countryside.

Sometime later, chilled and shivering with anxiety, I managed to force myself back inside and into the driver's seat. With my head out the window; freezing and gasping for air, I drove the next eighty miles in a complete state of panic. If I could just make it home to my family, surely this mysterious and frightening attack would come to an end. My concerned wife, Kathy, rushed out to greet me when I finally pulled into our driveway a day late and a few marbles short.

———

Being home didn't help. The attacks were frequent, and in between them, I lived in a constant state of anxiety. On several occasions, I found myself fleeing from otherwise harmless situations. Once, in a super market, I ran in a panic from a checkout stand. The puzzled checker watched me run as she continued dutifully to check my groceries. I never went back for them. Another day I got half a haircut. Simple things, such as getting caught in traffic, presented a major challenge for me. Fear was a constant threat if not a present enemy, and I felt like I was living in a continual fog.

How could this have happened to me, not only a Christian, but a former counselor and pastor? Really, what was the meaning of all of this? Who was I? Where was I going? All I knew was I was afraid.

What I didn't know was that God would step into my world with powerful answers to my agonizing questions; the same questions humankind has grappled with since the time of Eden.

PART TWO

As It Was In the Beginning

God the Father "birthed" us in his likeness
to share the awesome dynamic
of life at its fullest.

Chapter 2

A New Father

Then God said, "Let us make man in our image, in our like-ness." … So God created man in his own image, in the image of God he created him; male and female he created them.… The Lord God formed the man from the dust of the ground and breathed into his nostrils the breath of life, and man became a living being.
— Genesis 1:26-27 and 2:7

———

We live on a planet filled with people — parents and children who make up generations. Have you ever wondered why people exist? Why did God create all of us characters, anyway? Why did he want us? Based on strong evidence from Scripture, some of which we'll investigate in another chapter, I believe God created us, first, because he simply wanted the experience of having and raising his own children.

Second, I believe the unselfish Creator wanted others, birthed "in his own image," to experience the incredible sensation of *being*. He wanted children who would forever share with him in the awesome dynamic of life.

So one day, back in the beginning, after a new environment had been prepared, there was birthed a special, new kind of creation. Scripture records that up until then, God had only *spoken* when he created; this time it was much different, much more personal. This time he became intimately involved in the shaping and birthing of his creation. It went something like this …

As all the angels watched, the Creator slowly knelt down on one knee over a select piece of ground. With both hands and great care, he began to pull earth together. The form he brought to shape was maybe five or six feet long, just about a foot to a foot and a half wide, and ten inches or so high.

With both hands, he skillfully layered fine strands of hair on the top of the form. With his thumbs, he fashioned its eyebrows, its cheekbones, its chin. With unsurpassed craftsmanship and tenderness, he contoured its shoulders and every other striking line from the top of its beautiful head to the bottom of its beautiful feet.

An angel's whisper pierced the silence: "It looks like HIM!"

For fifteen seconds, a chorus of affirmative whispers swept the skies; then, all at once, they hushed. Silence governed the scene again as this new father leaned over the form and gently breathed into its nostrils "the breath of life." All heaven was astounded — a son was born! In short order, excitement charged the hemispheres a second time as the first parent brought to life his very first daughter!

Now *this* was incredible! *This* was significant! The Creator of all things had created "the significant." Mirrored in his image and likeness; unlike anything he had ever created before, these were *his children*. These were the children of God!

———

"It's a girl, Mr. Graham; your wife had a baby girl." The sudden announcement came from a nurse silhouetted in the open doorway leading to the brightly-lit delivery room beyond. "Would you like to see your wife and baby, Mr. Graham? Mr. Graham?"

"Pardon me, ma'am?" I responded, bewildered. *Baby? Why, that would make me — a dad!* There was an amused smile on the nurse's round, pleasant face. It was obvious she was experienced with "post-first-birth syndrome." With a subtle grin, she repeated herself, "Would you like to see your wife and baby, Mr. Graham?" Not wanting her to have too much fun at my expense, I confidently replied, "Oh … okay … uh … sure … can I?"

In what must have been record time, I donned the stylish anti-germ garb and nervously followed the rather humored pediatric nurse down the hallway toward the room. *It's a girl!* I thought. *I have a daughter! I'm a father!* My mind was jumping with joyful confusion. *Is this for real?* I asked myself. No answer. My smiling friend led me around a corner, stopped, and pointed at the bed where Kathy was resting. Kathy's eyes welled with tears as she turned to look at me. There was a smile on her face too; a beautiful smile. In her arms she cradled a small, blanketed baby — *our* baby, Michelle!

My heart was in my throat as Kathy lifted her towards me. I couldn't believe it. Ever since I was a young boy, I dreamed of having a family of my own, and here I was, many years later, holding my daughter; and she was beautiful.

———

Now, once more, please look back with me to that scene "in the beginning."

In that quiet place, still kneeling over each of his children, the loving Father leaned in close and gently breathed life into them. Overflowing with emotion and tenderness, he *kissed* his new son and daughter on their cheeks.

You might ask, "David, just what makes you think that's how it happened?" Well, that's easy. You see, I'm a dad. The good side of my "dadness" comes from him, and that's what I would have done; that's what I did. And our perfect, loving Father in heaven feels so much more about us than any earthly dad can feel.

The first Father is the same today as he was in Eden. His feelings still run deep, and he's pleased to be *our* Father.

Chapter 3

To Life!

I have come that they may have life, and have it to the full.
— John 10:10

———

*W*hat an incredible thing it is to have life, the ultimate existence! Think about it longer. To be a living, freethinking, creative being — this is no small matter. This existing is significant! The alternative to existing is not existing. This is not as good.

No doubt there are some who may differ with me on this "existing" point. Having counseled many hundreds of people over three-plus decades, and having walked through the slums of underdeveloped, and even developed nations, I am not unaware of the heartache and tragedy that intrude on human existence. My own emotional collapse left me questioning the goodness of existence. But this, in fact, is exactly the reason I'm writing. It was as a result of a much-needed confrontation with hidden insecurities — squatters in my own emotional slum — that I rediscovered the goodness of existence, of life.

Now, I'd like to ask those of you who are feeling low — and those of you who aren't — to simply keep an open mind. I'm really praying (and that's a fact) you will soon gain a life-changing perspective and fresh new zeal for this thing called *life*.

Life! The dynamic of life is incredible — an absolutely unbelievable gift. For God, our heavenly Parent, to include others in the experience of living, of being, was a tremendous demonstration of unselfish generosity and love. I believe today God wants us to experience — within healthy borders — the fascinating pleasures of feeling, laughing, loving, learning, reasoning, focusing, designing, inventing, exploring, building, entertaining and being entertained, teaching, and on and on. I'm convinced athletics, drama, dance, music, the fine arts, the sciences, technology, business, economics, and much, much more were all part of God's venue long before his children arrived. I'm also convinced his children will experience this same dynamic of life in heaven — with a wow factor!

All these creative activities exist in their ultimate form as part of his "life stuff," and it's all stuff he wants us to enjoy with him. "The earth is the Lord's, and everything in it" (Psalm 24:1). The earth is his, but he wanted to share it with us, and according to the first chapter in the Scriptures, he even instructed his children to rule over it: "God blessed them and said to them, 'Be fruitful and increase in number; fill the earth and subdue it. Rule over the fish of the sea and the birds of the air and over every living creature that moves on the ground'" (Genesis 1:28). His children were given the position of primary caretakers of the entire world. Life came with a pretty significant purpose.

I don't believe God wanted religion; he wanted relationship. He wanted to experience life with his children and for his children to experience and enjoy life with him. A completely fulfilling life was his original intention for us, and then, in time, his *redemptive* intention. As Jesus said, "I have come that they (we) may *have life and have it to the full.*"

Nothing brings the Father more satisfaction than connecting with us and seeing us live up to all we were created to be. He is the first and ultimate parent, and he loves to watch his children learn, grow, create, benefit from good choices, feel fulfilled, and experience personal happiness. He loves to see us *live*. How do I know this? As I told you — I'm a dad.

I'd like to again illustrate this parental perspective with another personal story. As I do, remember: Since man and woman's positive feelings and emotions were "created in God's own likeness," the positive side of "parentness" is truly a mirror of God's "parentness." This means the loving feelings good parents have for their children are actually an image of the loving feelings the most loving parent, God, has for each of us. And why do good parents want their children to have a good life? It's because that's what the Father in heaven wants. Think about that for a second while I turn back the clock to, well, a while ago.

———

These particular memories begin at our family home in Montana at the time when our first son, Jeff, was about two years old.

On the evening this story takes place, baby Mikey, as I recall, was already asleep in his crib, and the girls were playing quietly in their room. Kathy was doing the dishes, and I was recovering from giving Jeff Boy a bath. I finished drying him off, executed our ceremonial towel snap, and coerced the giggling little bug into his "jams."

In typical fashion, just as I pulled up his britches, he escaped. Somehow he thought he could provoke me into a chase, but my bath-soaked shirt and the wind-chill factor discouraged my pace. Instead, I moseyed down the hallway, crossed the living room and, to warm up, took a well-earned seat on the hearth of our brick fireplace.

Jeff Boy stopped circling the living room upon discovery of a rather large mound of tightly-folded and rounded pairs of socks on the coffee table. Kathy hadn't had the time to put all the laundry away earlier, and there sat the socks, just waiting for someone to notice them. Curious, Jeff edged over to the coffee table, stared at the socks, then turned with a smile to look at me.

Now, having been a father already for some time, I understood this particular look to mean two things. The first was: *Look, Daddy, at this wonderful thing I've found!* The second was: *Does my interest in this thing meet with your approval?* Not being able to stop myself, I smiled ever so slightly. Interpretation: *Approval granted.* His smile got bigger.

Not wanting to take this gift of approval for granted but willing to stretch his luck, the little boy moved his tiny hand in the direction of the stack and held it in the air about two inches over the top-most pair of socks. With his hand still suspended, he turned his head again to look at me. This meant: *How'm I doin' so far?*

My effort to respond with a stern look of warning failed. Frustrated by my lack of control, I struggled to hold back a grin. Jeff Boy picked up on it immediately. Interpretation: *Go for it!* Big, big smile.

Not allowing me and my facial expressions a second chance, the boy dropped his hand onto the stack and, with great glee, batted the once-neat pile over the entire surface of the coffee table until every last pair of socks fell tragically to the carpet below. All the while, Jeff smirked and laughed, glancing at me several times for further affirmation. I held my hands over my mouth to hide my smile, but somehow he still knew he was safe. With all the socks on the floor, he also knew he was successful. He had conquered the thing — and right in front of Dad.

Thoroughly entertained by all this creativity, I got an idea. Hmmm. While Jeff Boy continued to giggle over his triumph, I left my post, stole toward the coffee table unnoticed, and hid a single pair of the defeated socks (no pun intended) under my wet shirt. Then I slipped back, tongue in cheek, to the fireplace.

Upon arrival at the hearth, I turned around and, in an ascending, higher-than-normal voice, sang out, "Jeff Boy! Oh, *Jeff Boy!*" The first Jeff Boy got his attention and, on the second, I revealed my ammo. That's right; I wound up and fired the round ball of socks right at my little boy's stomach. After a moment of shock, he burst (figuratively speaking) into a squeal of laughter, which made me laugh until it almost hurt! This was great. I loved this. I loved this so much I grabbed three more pairs of socks.

I missed him on the second shot, and it landed across the room under the piano; but I nailed him on the next two, the first one hitting him on the shoulder, the second one right on the nose. This was too much fun! So I gathered all the rest of the socks in my arm and, one by one, unloaded on the now-moving target.

With both of us laughing hysterically, he ran and I threw until I was all out of ammo and there were at least three pairs of socks in every corner of the room. Those not out of sight were spread artistically everywhere else.

Now, really hurting, something caught me mid-laugh. Jeff Boy bent to the floor. With his own little hand, *he* picked up a pair of socks. I was stunned. With a great big, determined smile on his face, he rose to a cannon-like position. "Jeff Boy?" I queried, "What are you doing, Jeff Boy?"

His eyes were as happy as I had ever seen them as he looked first at me, then down at the ball of socks he was holding with his short little fingers. Then he looked at me again. I stood now, mouth open, watching in utter amazement as Jeff Boy began to swing his arms in a *perfect* pitching motion. With the look of Nolan Ryan, the boy wound up and fired what, without exaggeration, must have been at least, uhhh … a 105-mile-an-hour sock ball!

Miraculously, I somehow caught and protected myself from the flaming sock ball — a perfect strike! *What had I just witnessed?* Speechless, I dropped into a catcher's squat and rolled the ball of socks back in Jeff's direction.

"Throw it again, Jeff! Put it right in here!"

Again the kid wound up and, with fluid motion, hurled a hummer across the imaginary plate! My hands flinched with pain, but I didn't care. I quickly rolled the thing back again to Jeff.

"Down the pipe, Jeff, right here, right here!" (This is appropriate catcher talk.)

Once more, smiling proudly, he rocked; he fired! Sssshhoowoppp! Steeeeeeeerike! This was all unbelievable. I was dazed. So much so I lost all contact with reality and yelled, "Kathy, honey, come in here and look at this!"

As fast as reality left me, it returned. *What was I thinking?* As Kathy rounded the kitchen corner with a dish and towel in hand, my eyes scanned the formerly-neat living room, and in my panic, I searched for a believable excuse. Her eyes scanned the living room too.

"Honey," I said lovingly, honorably. "Uhhhh, Jeff got a little carried away here … butIpromisetocleanitallupinasec!" I had learned at times like this to run all my words together really fast as a diversion and then change the subject. "Honey, watch what *my* son can do. Okay, son, show your mom what you can do. Rock and fire, Jeff; rock and fire!"

With a motion of brilliance befitting a pro, the two year old put everything in it and threw a sizzler. I looked to Kathy, beaming. With no more than an "um hmm" and no change of expression, she simply turned around and walked back into the kitchen. *What? Didn't she see it? Couldn't she recognize greatness in its early stages?*

On a Saturday morning six years later, Jeff walked alone from the dugout to the pitcher's mound for the very first time. In his brand new K-Mart cleats, his cap pulled down over his ears, *my son* strode with confidence to the center of the diamond to pitch the Pee Wee season opener.

As I sat focused on the boy, my nose stuck in the backstop, I thought back to that eventful night in our living room six years before. I thought about all the early summer evenings afterward when Jeff, his little brother, Mikey, and I threw things at each other into the night. Tennis balls, pine cones — any object worked as long as it could be thrown and, without much damage, caught.

And now, here was one of *my* sons, all on his own, standing on the mound and rubbing up the baseball. He even spit. It was wonderful — a father's dream come true. Then the moment came; Jeff bent over and stared toward home plate. He looked scary — just like I taught him. The batter tensed up. Jeff wound up and fired a fast ball down the middle of the plate; fifteen seconds later, another! After the third pitch, I heard a loud sssshhoowoppp! followed by two of the most spiritual words a pitcher's dad can hear:

"Steeeeeeeeeeeerike threeeeeeeeeeee!" And a mom and dad got a life — at least a dad did.

Nine years later, at the age of seventeen, Jeff was asked to represent the Pacific Northwest as one of sixteen high school and college players selected from five different states to play baseball in the Pan Pacific Games in Brisbane, Australia. Jeff had a great experience, and his team took the championship.

A few months after the Australia trip, I walked the one hundred and fifty yards to our mailbox and found a videotape of the Brisbane games sent by Jeff's coach. With speed I thought I had lost, I raced to the house and straight to the VCR. Sitting on the floor with tears in my eyes, I watched my *son* step to the plate, and I thought … of socks.

This is just one father's perspective, but it is not unlike our heavenly Father's. The only difference is he's a *perfect* father. While the things of earth attempt to drag us down, our Father is forever attempting to lift us up. If everyone else turns against us, he's the one who'll still be standing by our side — and he loves being there by *your* side.

Maybe you are a Christian who really loves God and tries so hard to please him but are never sure if you do. Even though you may not always feel like a champion, he loves and believes in you. He wants you to have *life*.

And for others of you who are open and searching, the Father wants to encourage you. He loves to see your earnest heart. He welcomes your questions — *all* your questions. You have extremely great worth. God longs for you to have life as it was meant to be. He is your greatest fan, and he loves you more than you could ever imagine.

Chapter 4

Mirrors

Father,… this is eternal life: that they may know you.
— John 17:1, 3

———

*P*icture yourself at the creation scene in Eden, and pretend for a moment you're Adam or Eve. You've just taken your very first breath of air while lying on your back in this beautiful garden. You're experiencing consciousness for the very first time in your life — this is the "first time" in your life. Are you imagining this? Interesting feeling, isn't it? You will note, as you imagine this, that you have absolutely no clue what's going on. You have no idea who you are, where you've come from, or where you're going. Without further information at this point, you might soon be tempted to experience your very first panic attack. You're beginning to sense the need for reassurance.

Suddenly, you feel someone touching your hands — at least you think they're your hands. You've never experienced touch before. But before you can process this, you feel yourself being pulled up and forward into a sitting position. You just have to look. Without knowing how, you make your eyelids open. Now things really get interesting. If you knew how to speak, you might ask, "What on earth?" — which would be a good question.

There, before your eyes, is the most amazing thing you've ever seen — the *only* thing you've ever seen: the face of your Father. The confusion and insecurity germinating inside you begin to fade. His radiant eyes and joyful smile somehow convince your brand new emotions he loves you and is deeply pleased with you.

He leans forward, gathers you in his strong arms, and hugs you with tenderness and honor. He somehow conveys, in your very first hearing, who you are and where you've come from. Your breathing slows; you're feeling safe. He calls you son, or daughter, and you're feeling very, very significant.

———

Two of man's most basic needs are affirmation and information. Love and knowledge are among the essential ingredients necessary to maintain a strong sense of well-being and significance (healthy self-worth). Children need to be loved and mentored to properly grow into their significant selves.

In his book *Healing the Shame That Binds You*, John Bradshaw paraphrases psychologist and psychoanalyst Erik Erikson with these words:

> We needed to know from the beginning that we could trust the world. The world came to us in the form of our primary care-takers. We needed to know that we could count on someone outside of us to be there for us in a humanly predictable manner. If we had a caretaker who was mostly predictable, and who touched us and mirrored all our behaviors, we developed a sense of basic trust. When security and trust are present, we begin to develop an interpersonal bond, which forms a bridge of *mutuality*. Such a bridge is crucial for the development of self-worth. The only way a child has of developing a sense of self is through a relationship with another. We are "we" before we are "I". In this early stage of life, we can only know

ourselves in the *mirroring eyes* of our primary caretakers. Each of us needed a relational bridge with our primary caretaker in order to grow. (Emphases added.)

In the same way, as I discussed in chapter three, it was the Father's original and redemptive intention that all the adult children of the earth experience the utmost in security and significance. This can only happen through a bonded relationship with him, the *ultimate* caregiver. As with little children, we bigger children must have this mutuality, or "we-ness" with the Father, in order to experience *ultimate* individuality.

We know few details of the first couple or the length of their time in Eden, but we can be certain Adam and Eve's bond to the ultimate Caregiver afforded these first two children the greatest security and self-worth possible. The creation account says: "and *they were not ashamed*" (Genesis 2:25).

We've already noted that Adam and Eve were given an extremely important responsibility. What an honor to be assigned the role of stewards of the earth!

Indeed, these first children experienced the *ultimate sense of significance* by virtue of their *significant mutuality with their Father* and their *significant well-being and purpose*. This just had to be life at its very best.

Using another family story, I'd like to illustrate the dynamic of mutuality. A side note here: I know it's a little risky for a parent, in this case a dad, to carry on about his children. I'm taking a chance because I believe God has often been misrepresented and is seldom portrayed as a loving parent. My reason for telling parent-children stories is to illustrate in a small way how the Father in heaven feels for his children in a *big* way.

———

Kimi had always been a happy, carefree little girl growing up. She had a contentment about her that made others feel contented too. She seldom ever asked for anything, but when she did, it was her smile that would get to me, perhaps because, like her heart, it was so genuinely innocent. Now a mature young woman of seventeen,

Kimberly was walking gracefully across the stage, disarming an audience with the same beautiful smile that had so often taken advantage of her father's soft heart. She wore a burgundy formal, and long blond curls graced her shoulders. I thought she was gorgeous.

It was June of 1988, and the occasion was Montana's annual America Junior Miss Program held in Butte, Montana. Kathy and I were thrilled when, a few months earlier, Kimi had won the title of Kalispell Junior Miss. Now she was competing against girls from all around the state. We'd been told nearly twenty thousand young women from across the nation enter the program each year. Ultimately, only fifty are chosen, one from each state, to compete in the America Junior Miss Program staged in Mobile, Alabama.

About twenty teenage girls, as I recall, crossed the stage that Saturday night in the culmination of a full, grueling week of interviews and rehearsals. Kimi was now moving toward the microphone for her introduction. Given the fact that parents in these kinds of settings are basically weird, you'll understand when I say, "She was awesome!" Grace, beauty, and charm (plus some traits inherited from Kathy's side of the family) all in one, Kimi was wonderful, and we just stared at her. When she finished speaking, she looked over at us. Our glistening eyes and broad smiles told her, "Way to go, sweetheart!"

As the evening went along, the girls were each judged on their performances in numerous categories. Then the moment came for the five finalists to be selected. The audience erupted into applause as the first teen was announced. The elated young lady stepped forward from the large semicircle of contestants to take her position center stage. Finalists two, three, and four responded to their call until there was only one girl left to be announced. There was a deliberate pause from the master of ceremonies before he finally declared: "And the fifth finalist is … Kimberly Graham!"

We were overwhelmed. "She's a finalist, honey! She's a finalist!" I cried, as I grabbed Kathy's hand.

The room buzzed; giggles and laughter spiced the air, and tension mounted as the judges retreated to their chamber to make their final decision.

After nearly an hour, the judges reentered the auditorium. When they did, the five finalists returned to center stage. The emcee took the envelope from the judges and, rather dramatically, returned to his podium. After the necessary acknowledgements, the man opened the first envelope.

The fourth runner-up was announced, and Kimberly was still standing there. The third and then the second runners-up were announced, and our Kimi was still standing there, one of two remaining finalists. The crowd went into a squealing-while-you-wait mode — or perhaps it was just Kathy; I'm not sure. I just remember my heart was in up-tempo.

While we were aging from anticipation, the emcee did an annoying thing: he spent forever telling what the winner would win. *Yeah, whatever,* I thought. *WHO WON?*

And finally:

"Now, it is my privilege to introduce this year's Montana Juuuuunior Miss ..."

Yes, yes, I stewed, squeezing Kathy's hand tighter. *Go on, go onnnnnn!*

"... Kalispell's KIMBERLY GRAHAM!"

"What? Honey, what did he say?" I asked. Kathy couldn't answer; she was crying. I never would have cried if she hadn't cried. The place filled with screams. The applause went on as *our* little girl took a bouquet of roses in arm and walked beautifully, tearfully down-stage to stand before the audience. After a minute of standing ovation, she turned around, and all the contestants raced to her, jumping at her side and giving her big hugs.

Congratulations, tears, more hugs ... Oh, what a night! I ran to a telephone, bursting with pride, to tell family and friends Kimi was going to Alabama.

———

A month later, Kimberly boarded a plane to the beautiful Gulf Coast city of Mobile for two weeks of glorious festivities and more grueling rehearsals leading up to the national America Junior Miss Program. Fifty Girl Scout troops (one for each state winner), the mayor, other dignitaries, a brass band, and TV news cameras were waiting at the airport to meet and interview each girl as she stepped off the plane.

Parents of the contestants weren't allowed to have contact with their daughters during the first week of program activities, so Kathy and I didn't arrive until week two. There were only two times parents could see their daughters during that second week, and then only in a group with the other contestants and their parents. We got to meet up with Kimi once at an afternoon outing at the beach, and a second time at a special evening outdoor barbeque and hoe-down. While each event was really special, just being together was enough.

On the final Saturday night of the program, thousands of people crowded the streets as fifty of America's finest young women were paraded through downtown Mobile. Each contestant was seated up high on the back seat of her own antique convertible, the name of her state posted on the front grille of the car. Each girl waved to the cheering fans as her driver slowly cruised to the front entrance of the grand old Saenger Theater.

As Kimi's car came near where we stood waiting, I began waving my arms in the air, hoping she'd see us.

"Kimi!" I yelled.

I'll never forget the moment when her eyes met ours. Her smile got huge … ours got bigger. Her eyes got a little teary … ours got a lot.

"We love you, honey! We *love* you!" I shouted above the crowd noise as we waved her out of sight.

———

Many years have passed since that memorable night. Although a few state directors told us they thought Kimberly would be a finalist, she didn't reach the final five in Mobile. What the directors didn't realize, however, was she had already reached *our* final four — she was one of our children, and, like her sister and brothers, we were always proud of who she was.

Most important, Kimberly never doubted it. She told me years later those brief visits with us leading up to the big night were the highlights of her Junior Miss experience.

"I was a little girl," she said, "1800 miles away from home and pressed into a challenging situation with total strangers. I was nervous and exhausted, but most of all, lonely.

"You know, Daddy," she went on, "loneliness can often be most intense in a crowd, in a sea of people you don't know. All of a sudden, you and Mom were there with me on my journey, sharing a picnic lunch on a beach; hugging at a square dance. You were my symbol of normalcy; you brought me comfort and assurance. And I was okay.

"What carried me through was you constantly telling me you were proud of me. You affirmed me, and nothing else mattered, not even how I finished in the program. What I saw on your faces as you stood there in the crowd that night were the unspoken words that made me comfortable in my own skin when I walked into the Saenger Theater."

We have loved helping our children experience life. It's been a privilege to be their "mirrors" and help them grow to know themselves for who they are. Even though they haven't always made perfect choices or had success, they've remained connected to us in the safety of a loving, mutual relationship. They've found significance, well-being, and purpose in our common bond. They're our sons and daughters. We'll never stop loving them, and we're very proud of them.

This is the way it is supposed to be. This is how it is in the Father's house.

PART THREE

The Way Back

The children need their Father
to restore their significance and security.

Chapter 5

So What on Earth's the Matter?

Formerly, when you did not know God, you were slaves to those who by nature are not gods.
— Galatians 4:8

———

What went wrong in Eden?

———

Many good people resist this idea, but it's my belief that we humans, birthed by our Creator and Caregiver, are still dependents by nature. In the same way children are dependent upon and in need of their caregivers' proper leadership to reach successful adulthood, so I'm convinced we are still dependent upon and in need of a higher authority — a *perfect* caregiver — in order to reach and maintain our full potential in our "human-beingness."

Even as a great invention requires the continued care of its inventor in order to achieve its full potential, so we require the continual and devoted care of our creator Father to achieve and keep our ultimate state of completion and significance. The big difference, of course, between human beings and inventions is humans have been given the privilege of free will. We have the power to make independent choices, including those of an independent lifestyle — but we will *still* remain vulnerable and dependent.

Now, let's recall the temptation recorded in the third chapter of Genesis, particularly verse five, where the Serpent says, "When you eat of it (the fruit) your eyes will be opened, and you will be like God." I call this line "hell's horrendous hoax." As I've said, it's through dependence within a perfect mutuality that one experiences the greatest in beingness. Here we have a lying, diabolical power tempting the dependents to cross the safe borders of their mutuality, convincing them that by taking a position of *independence* they would be much better off and would gain much greater significance. Sounds suspiciously like the motives behind modern day temptations.

In his extreme jealousy over the loss of his own heavenly mutuality, Satan, the now-enemy of God, was purposely prodding the children into his own misery where they would not only keep him company but also experience his dominating abuse. In Genesis 2:25, Adam and Eve, though they were both naked, felt no shame. However, in Genesis 3:7-10, after their departure from perfect relationship, "they realized they were naked ... and they hid (in fear) from the Lord God" having experienced their first encounter with shame. Adam and Eve simply and tragically shifted their dependence away from perfect mutuality to a dark one. They traded in the good for the terrible, the loving for the hostile.

The apostle Paul speaks of the consequences of this shift in mutuality in his New Testament letter to the Christians at Ephesus when he says, "You once followed the ways of this world and of the ruler of the kingdom of the air, the spirit who is now at work in those who are disobedient ... Like the rest, we were by nature *objects of wrath*" (Ephesians 2:2-3). All mankind had fallen into the snare of a hostile relationship.

The apostle John, in his first letter, writes: "The whole world is under the control of the evil one" (1 John 5:19). Whether or not you are one who considers the Bible a conclusive source of authority, I think you would agree this world is pretty dysfunctional. There's some force behind all this, messing things up. Many would say it's downright scary. In every nation there is a cry for peace and safety.

The answer? I believe it is found in the proclamations of Christ, which clearly convey we must have a renewed dependency upon the original and ultimate Parent. Jesus said to call him Father.

Many who consider themselves to be independent people might, for good reasons, take exception to the word *dependence*. For many, words like dependence and submission have the very unfriendly ring of devaluing control. Unpleasant memories of experiences with less-than-fully-functional caregivers, dehumanizing relationships, and demeaning environments are what most disappointed people are trying to escape.

It is subjection to unhealthy control, after all, that does some of the greatest damage to one's well-being and self-worth. Many who have suffered neglect, dishonor, and abuse at the hands of earthly care-givers avoid any relationship with authority figures. They think they will be safer if they can be their own final authority.

My point, however, is this: Because of our dependent nature, mutuality of *some* kind is unavoidable. With our free will, we can choose to place our dependency upon our Creator/Caregiver, or, either willingly or by default, we end up placing our dependency on some *other* power.

———

Outside of Eden, it would *seem* we are destined to remain finite, limited human beings potentially subject to an unlimited number and variety of powerful dominators. In an attempt to avoid domination, we often adopt a survivalist mentality. We tend to gravitate into unhealthy survival camps. Here are three I recognize ...

The first one I call "Camp Independence." This camp is made up of those who want to steer clear of people in general, retreating into more private and non-conformist lifestyles. I'm thinking there may have been a few grizzled mountain men who set up camp in this camp. Even in misery, these folks don't love or need much company. This camp's motto could easily be "No one's gonna tell *me* what to do!" or "Keep out! Beware of dogs!"

The second camp I call "Camp Macho-ism." Although there are varying degrees of macho-ism, the main objective of the members in this camp is to be more powerful, to survive by being "the fittest," to conquer rather than be conquered, and so on. Unfortunately, "he who lives by the sword, dies by the sword," which, for the record, Jesus said. This camp's motto might be, "The end justifies the means" or "Show no mercy!"

Human history provides us with unlimited examples of those who lean toward the macho side. One of my past favorites was Muhammad Ali, the former and three-time Heavy Weight Champion of the World. I actually really liked this guy — but not as much as he liked himself. He will go down in boxing history not only for being the greatest, but for *saying* he was "the greatest" on many occasions.

I heard an interesting story (don't know if it's true) about Ali during his heyday that demonstrates the deception of macho-ism. As the story goes, the Champ, on his way to do battle, was sitting in the first class section (where else?) of a plane that was just moving into its take-off position. As the big DC 10 turned to begin its charge down the runway, the attendant kindly but firmly said to the Champ, "Mr. Ali, Sir, you don't have your seat belt on!" Always known to be quick on his feet, he retorted with a smile of genius on his face, "Huh, Superman doesn't need a seat belt." The sweet attendant, even quicker on *her* feet, said, "But Mr. Ali, Sir … Superman doesn't need an airplane."

Macho-ism has its limitations.

We may have the power to dominate for a season at a certain level, but sooner or later the nature of our dependency and vulnerability will deliver us up to an unfriendly, more powerful force. Death, for example, has a convincing way of dominating even the most macho.

The third major group I call "Camp Mouse-ism." It's made up of members whose objective it is to lay low, follow the line of least resistance, and avoid a fight at all costs. In hopes of evading conflict, the person with more submissive tendencies may often feign weakness so as not to pose a threat to the macho world. He or she finds some strange sense of identity and security by adopting the profile of the forever-victim — the "doormat." My mind's a blank at the moment when it comes to stories about members of Camp Mouse-ism. They're usually not mountain men, super heroes, unlikeable bosses, or braggers. The third camp's motto could be, "I'm sorry, I'm sorry!" or "I'm so stupid."

These three camps are adequately represented within and without the religious world.

It comes as a surprise to many I have talked to, especially those who may have been subjected to strict legalism or religiosity, that being in a place of dependence upon God is not about being manipulated or controlled. On the contrary, being submitted to our Father, the ultimate caregiver, means the discovery of *true* freedom and the meaning of life!

Sadly, many Christians haven't understood and therefore haven't enjoyed the very essence of Christianity. Far too many good people continue to faithfully sing the hymns, heed the rules (or try to), bless the food, and pay the tithes more out of subconscious duty or fear than out of the happiness found in the supreme mutuality. Though their lifestyle is "spiritual," they often are still more affected by some past or present unloving mutuality rather than by the Loving One. They are more influenced by their memories than by the faith they profess. Many are further confused by the misconception that God is primarily a judge who isn't all that loving.

These good people do all they know to do and yet are still not benefiting from the ultimate bond with the Father, which was the primary objective of his entire redemptive strategy. Unaware of the wonderful new provision of loving mutuality, they continue to experience insecurity and insignificance even as they struggle against both in one of the survival camps.

So, what on earth's the matter? The matter is this: Mutuality, the most important link to life, is missing. The children — of all ages — need their Father!

Chapter 6

The Phenomenal Exchange

Christ Jesus …, being in very nature God, did not consider
equality with God something to be grasped, but made himself
nothing, taking the very nature of a servant, being made in
human likeness. And being found in appearance as a man, he
humbled himself and became obedient to death — even death
on a cross!
— Philippians 2:5-8

*T*he word *gospel* means good news. Most Christians know this, but it's amazing to me so many really don't understand what the "good news" is. I, too, was once in this place. The good news is a declaration of restored mutual relationship between the Father and his children! How was all this made possible? God, the Significant, became insignificant so we might become significant again. By leaving his place of authority in the kingdom of heaven and becoming a servant on earth, Jesus Christ relinquished his position and inheritance so we, the lost children, could have our position and inheritance restored! I call this "the phenomenal exchange of significance."

Think about it: The Creator of the world and the entire universe; the One who came up with everything from DNA to dinosaurs and all those other mysterious and wonderful things that amaze — this is the One who *voluntarily became a human baby birthed by and under the care of a teenage girl* in a stable behind a modest local inn in a small town called Bethlehem. Incredible.

Jesus became vulnerably dependent to pay the price for mankind's wrongful attempt at independence. He became human to suffer an inhumane death. When he completed his sacrificial, passionate objective, the Scriptures tell us: "God exalted him to the highest place and gave him the name that is above every name, that at the name of Jesus every knee should bow, in heaven and on earth and under the earth, and every tongue confess that Jesus Christ is Lord, to the glory of God the Father" (Philippians 2:9-11). Not only that, Ephesians 2:6 says further: "God *raised us up* with Christ and *seated us* with him in the heavenly realms in Christ Jesus."

Do you see how greatly we have been honored? Because of Christ's most loving and unselfish mission, we are seated alongside him as both his brothers and sisters *and* the honored children of God!

———

The love the Father in heaven has for *all* people is way beyond our capacity to understand. In an act that caused him extreme grief, he literally sent his cherished Son to hell — for *us*. It was a huge and costly love; the greatest expression of love in the history of the world. So what does this mean in the here and now? It means the Father and his Son think *you*, my friend, are extremely valuable.

What a Father! What a Son!

On earth, Jesus walked and talked his relationship with his Father in everything he did, but never in exclusive terms. The purpose of his continual references to the heavenly Father was to reveal to all his followers that *they were included* in the relationship. This is why he specifically told them to address God as *our* Father.

Since God is *our* Father, we no longer have to strive for identity or significance. These are absolutely ours, a result of the great exchange, when we make the choice to enter back into loving mutuality with him. Jesus illustrated this in my favorite parable, that of the prodigal son, in Luke 15:11-31. The major message in the parable starts in verse twenty. After experiencing the consequences of his choices for complete independence and selfish living, the shame-filled son returns in true humility to his former country and his father. Listen to this profound verse:

"But while he was still a long way off, his father saw him and was filled with compassion for him; he *ran* to his son, threw his arms around him and kissed him. (Imagine this kind of reception — the kind that's ahead for everyone who takes the road home.) The son said to him, 'Father, I have sinned against heaven and against you. I am no longer worthy to be called your son.'"

Now look at loving mutuality in action in verse twenty-two. Without hesitation, the father joyfully shouts a command to reinstate the son to his former position of dignity: "Quick! Bring the *best robe* and put it on him. Put a *ring* on his finger (think about that — a ring and a robe: eternal commitment and covering!) and sandals on (protection for) his feet.... Let's have a feast and celebrate. For this son of mine was dead and is alive again; he was lost and is found."

This story carries some really important facts: First, the Father's love is big. Second, those who give up their own type of search and follow Christ down the road to the Father will find freedom from sadness and insecurity. The recovery of their stature as one of God's children will be made total and complete.

When we give up the lonely voyage in search of an independent self in the cold sea of faulty pursuits, and when we fully place our innate dependency upon the Father, we can finally experience the home he's longed for us to have — and he can finally experience the children he's longed to have back home.

Jesus made it all happen. The exchange has taken place. The Significant leads us home to restore our identity, to re-establish *our* significance!

And he did this for *you*.

Chapter 7

The Spirit of Sonship

For you did not receive a spirit that makes you a slave again to fear, but you received the Spirit of sonship. And by him we cry, "Abba, Father." The Spirit himself testifies with our spirit that we are God's children.
— Romans 8:15-16

———

*T*he puff of smoke was followed instantly by the crack of the starter's gun. Standing at the finish line, my heart began to pound a little harder as I looked across the infield of the oval quarter-mile track to see Michael take the early lead in the two-hundred meter dash. As he rounded the turn and bolted down his lane, I fixed my camera on the boy's charging physique. Even through the viewfinder and over ninety yards away, I could see that familiar face tensed for speed and focused on its target with a heated look of determination. Using every ounce of strength and gram of desire, Michael stretched his lead in his sprint for the finish. As he leaned for the tape with his chest fully extended, I could hear an intense groan blasting out from somewhere deep inside his exhausted frame. Blinking back tears, I declared to myself, *That's my son!*

By now, I'm sure you have picked up on my theme regarding parents and the emotions they can feel for their children. Nearly every time I've told a story about one of our four, I've had a parent approach me saying something like, "Boy, I can sure identify with your stories about your kids. So many times I have felt the same way about my own children. Hearing your stories makes me want to be with them right now." This is usually where they tell me a great story of their own.

It's interesting the other kinds of reactions I'll get as well. Some parents will express deep regret over their lack of parenting skills and how they "wish they could only do it over again." Other times I encounter either a parent or a child who will express resentment or anger upon hearing stories about family due to painful memories of their own. I respect their feelings. Their memories and pain are real.

Thankfully, we can find genuine healing in spite of very sad memories. We'll talk more about this in a later chapter. May I just say for now, I believe as long as we're still alive it's not too late to experience real joy that can override unhappy memories.

Again, the point of all my stories is to illustrate that the Father has even deeper feelings for *his* children. He doesn't want religious subjects. He wants genuine relationship with healthy and happy sons and daughters!

I propose that what the Bible calls "sonship" (and "daughtership") is the very heart of the New Testament. Before I share another story, I'd like us to take a look at a sampling of verses showing just how key, how central, this subject of sonship and daughtership actually is. Let these ancient words from Scripture really sink in.

John 1:10-13 says: "He was in the world, and though the world was made through him, the world did not recognize him.... Yet to all who received him, to those who believed in his name, he gave the right to become *children of God* — *children* born not of natural descent, nor of human decision or a husband's will, but *born of God*."

Note here that John doesn't call us Christians; he calls us God's children. Remember, the sole purpose of God's redemptive mission on earth was to make us his children again. Just two chapters later, Jesus meets a religious leader named Nicodemus. Unlike other Pharisees Jesus encountered, this man seems to be an earnest seeker of truth.

THE SPIRIT OF SONSHIP

Jesus, seemingly out of context, brings up the topic of birth. Contemplate two things with me here. First, the verse we just read above states the reason he came into the world was so we could "be born as children of God." The second thing is, whenever there is a birth, there is always the involvement of at least two beings; there is always at least one parent and at least one child present. We've already termed this relationship *mutuality*. In his talk with Nicodemus, Jesus introduces the incredible advent of mutuality with God!

John 3:3-8 says: "I tell you the truth, no one can see the kingdom of God unless he is born again." Nicodemus responds: "How can a man be born when he is old? Surely he cannot enter a second time into his mother's womb to be born!" Jesus answers, "I tell you the truth, no one can enter the kingdom of God unless he is *born of water and the Spirit*." Jesus is making reference both to human birth into earthly mutuality (the word *water* here, I believe, is referring to the water of a mother's womb) and then spiritual birth into heavenly mutuality. This double meaning is further supported by what he says next: "*Flesh gives birth to flesh*, but the *Spirit gives birth to spirit*. You should not be surprised at my saying, 'You must be born again.'"

Jesus said we need to be born a *second* time, God's Spirit giving new birth to our spirits. What's the real significance of this? *Being born again means becoming a new, significant child validated forever under the loving care of the ultimate parent, Father God!* Sadly, many "born again" people can see themselves as "Christians," but can't see themselves as the Father's closest *relatives(!)* — his esteemed *sons* or *daughters*.

I call Romans 8 the sonship chapter. One of the most pivotal chapters in the New Testament, it holds a treasure of truth I believe often goes unnoticed. The entire chapter is loaded with importance, but I'll note just a few relevant points for now.

Romans 8:14-18 says: "Those who are led by the Spirit of God *are sons of God*. For you did not receive a spirit that makes you a slave again to fear, but you received the *Spirit of sonship*. And by him we cry 'Abba (which is the Greek word for *Daddy*), Father.' The Spirit himself testifies with our spirit that we are God's children. Now if *we are children*, then we are heirs — *heirs of God and co-heirs with Christ*, if indeed we share in his sufferings in order that *we may also share in his glory*."

Have you ever grasped this profound truth? Have you ever even been told that if you are reborn, as defined by Jesus, you have received the Spirit of *sonship?* The Spirit of sonship or the Spirit of daughtership is in you — in YOU! You have not received the spirit of "wormship," which degrades the work of Christ and the royal blood that flows through your veins. You have received the Spirit of *sonship.* This astounding fact gives you the distinctive position of heir, just like Christ, meaning you "may also share in his glory" — in his significance. If we are God's heirs, then we have a new heavenly stature and status. This should translate into an amazing new experience of inner peace and a wonderful sense of significance right here and now on earth.

Another fascinating thing about this revealing information is it's conveyed by Paul — former militant Pharisee, persecutor of Christians, and the man who prided himself in observing every relationally-distant letter of the law. Here is this character fresh out of "Camp Macho-ism" introducing the entire Greek and Hebrew world to the word *daddy!* The man who had people killed for speaking in intimate terms concerning God is now the first to introduce us to *Daddy* as an appropriate way to address God! Is this strange or what?

Although ironic, it is no accident God chose Paul to deliver the name *Daddy.* Paul was a perfect model of how the Father wants to set his children free from the bondage of religiosity and release them into the intimate dynamic of relationship. He set a Pharisee free and he sets *us* free through the Spirit of sonship.

———

Okay, I proposed earlier that sonship and daughtership is the very heart of the New Testament. Take a quick look with me at some other letters of Paul and his fellow Apostles that address the subject of the Father and his children:

· Romans 8:19-21:
> The creation waits in eager expectation for the **sons of God** to be revealed. For the creation was subjected to frustration, not by its own choice, but by the will of the one who subjected it, in hope that creation itself will be liberated from its bondage to decay and brought into the **glorious freedom of the children of God**. We know that the whole creation has been groaning as in the pains of childbirth right up to the present time.

· 2 Corinthians 6:18:

> "**I will be a Father to you, and you will be my sons and daughters**, says the Lord Almighty."

· Galatians 3:26 and 4:7:

> **You are all sons of God** through faith in Christ Jesus.... God sent his Son, born of a woman, born under law, to redeem those under law, **that we might receive the full rights of sons. Because you are sons, God sent the Spirit of his Son into our hearts, the Spirit who calls out, "*Abba*, Father." So you are no longer a slave, but a son; and since you are a son, God has made you also an heir.**

· Ephesians 2:18:

> "Through him we both (Jews and Gentiles alike) have access to the **Father by one Spirit**."

· 1 Peter 1:

> Praise be to God and the **Father** of our Lord Jesus Christ! In his great mercy **he has given us new birth** into a living hope through the resurrection of Jesus Christ from the dead, and into an **inheritance** that can never perish, spoil or fade — kept in heaven for you (v. 1-4). As obedient **children**, do not conform to ... evil desires (v. 14). Since you call on a **Father** ... (v. 17). For you have been **born again**, not of perishable seed but of imperishable (v. 23).

· 1 Peter 2:

> "Like **new born babies**, crave pure spiritual milk" (v. 2). "You are a chosen people, a royal priesthood, a holy nation, **a people belonging to God**" (v. 9). "Once you were not a people, but now you are **a people of God**" (v. 10).

· 1 John 3:1:

> "How great is the love **the Father** has lavished on us, that we should be called **children of God! And that is what we are!**"

· 1 John 5:19:

> "We know that **we are children of God**."

To conclude our Scripture search, I'd like to end with the words of Jesus found in the gospel of Mark, chapter 10, starting at verse 13:

> People were bringing little children to Jesus to have him touch them, but the disciples rebuked them. When Jesus saw this, he was indignant. He said to them, "Let the little children come to me, and do not hinder them, for the kingdom of God belongs to such as these. I tell you the truth, anyone who will not receive the kingdom of God **like a little child** will never enter it." And he took the children in his arms, put his hands on them and blessed them.

What does the Father want from us in response to his love and gift of son- and daughtership? It's very simple, really. He just wants us to become *like children* once again, not in the same degree of immaturity as a child, but in the same degree of dependency. He wants us to move into the safety of his arms and just let him be our Father.

———

I'll never forget the time when my son, Jeff, was just beginning to articulate his words. Actually, it was soon after the time of the sock incident. This particular event took place on a day when Kathy was very sick. For several days, Kathy had grown steadily more ill. Her fever continued to climb and her pain became more intense. It was getting to the point of becoming a serious matter.

After some time, I realized I had not taken the time to pray over Kathy. So I did. I went into our room where she was lying in bed, sat down carefully beside her, cleared my throat, and began to pray. It was a long prayer. I quoted Scriptures. Taking bits and pieces of learning from various spiritual periods in my life, I covered every doctrinal angle I could think of. First, I prayed, "Lord, if it be thy will, heal Kathy." Several phrases later, I prayed "in faith" as if to say, "Of course it's God's will." Finally, I "claimed her healing" and said, "Lord, heal Kathy." To be perfectly honest, I was never really sure what his will was, but I attempted to pray with as much spiritual correctness as I possibly could.

When I got all done with my "thorough" prayer, Kathy smiled patiently and then asked, "Honey, *now* would you take me to the hospital?"

I just stared at her.

Some moments later, Jeff Boy came waddling into the bedroom. First, he looked at me. Then he looked at his mommy. Then he looked at me again and asked in his tiny little voice, "Mommy sick?" I said, "Yes, Jeff Boy, Mommy is very sick."

After a thoughtful pause, I said, "Jeff Boy, would you like to pray for Mommy?" Folding my hands to add further meaning, I repeated myself again more slowly, "Want to *pray* for Mommy?"

Jeff looked up at me and replied, "Yup." He moved toward the edge of the bed while Kathy inched painfully to the same edge to greet her little boy.

I watched as my toddler son, with carefulness and confidence, stretched out his little arm and placed his soft palm on his mommy's hot forehead. In all my life I will never forget his exact words. He prayed: "God … bless this food. Amen."

(Long pause as I stare at Jeff.)

To my amazement, Kathy was *instantly healed!*

With a huge smile and sudden enthusiasm, she jumped out of bed and left the room in search of her vacuum cleaner. *What!?* I asked myself, at the same time watching my son as he waddled, straight-faced and ho hum, out of the bedroom following his mommy.

Sitting there on the bed, dazed and confused, I tried to figure out what had just happened. Maybe it had just taken God a little while to figure out *my* prayer … maybe. But I knew better.

"Uh, good prayer, Jeff Boy," I muttered reluctantly. I could just imagine a small gathering of angels chuckling amongst themselves over the whole incident.

———

In the same way Jeff felt safe and confident at home with his mom and dad, so our Father wants us — his children by the Spirit of sonship — to live safe and confident with him … in his house … forever.

Chapter 8

Holy Kid!

And by that will (his will), we have been made holy through the sacrifice of the body of Jesus Christ once for all.
— Hebrews 10:10

———

Not every family story can be a good one. All of my children, not to mention their parents, have made their share of mistakes. Human nature dictates that we will all make a poor choice sooner or later. I don't like choosing any one such incident because it means singling out one of the kids. This particular story, however, does serve a particular purpose in this particular chapter, and the particular kid in question gave me permission to tell it.

I need to begin by saying this kid is Michael, or Mikey as he's often affectionately referred to. Michael has more good qualities than you could count. Just to mention a few, he is loyal as a son, brother, and friend; thoughtful, kind, generous, and highly motivated. Somewhere on the quality list, I would have to include his willingness to take on a challenge. This boy has always loved a challenge, whether it was as a running back charging through 250-pound defensive linemen (Michael earned a first-team all-conference selection in high school football), charging up a rock cliff with ropes, or diving off a 100-foot bridge just for the thrill of it. His orientation towards a challenge has led him into some very interesting situations. One time it led him into a police station.

I remember this story taking place when Michael was eleven years old. I can remember his age because it happened only a week or so after he won a second place ribbon for his entry in the sixth grade countywide science fair. Science Fair night was really exciting. Michael had put a lot of effort into his project, and the ride home in the car was a happy one. I can still see him sitting tall in the passenger seat as we returned from his job well done.

About a week later, while entertaining guests on a late Sunday afternoon, I received a call. It was from a police officer at a nearby city hall. Michael, by the way, had ridden into town with older friends for an outing.

"Mr. Graham," said the officer, "I have a certain son of yours down here at the police station."

"You do?" I responded, clearing my throat.

"Yes. It seems your son, Michael, thought he needed some baseball cards and left one of our local stores without paying for them. He is being retained here at the station until you come and pick him up."

I waited for our guests to leave, reasoning that it would give Mikey a little extra time to think about his situation. Needless to say, I had extra time to think about his situation too.

After a couple of hours, I finally walked through the entry doors of the police station and up to the imposing police receptionist, who sat behind a heavily-barred window. Behind her, in a far corner, I could see Michael sitting, still and bent over, on a gray metal folding chair.

The woman officer slid some papers to me for my signature, one of which was a promise to bring Michael in to see a juvenile officer the following day. When I finished, I looked up to see the receptionist offer a surprisingly sweet smile followed by the words, "He really seems like a very good boy."

She pressed a button, setting off a loud buzzer indicating the giant prisoner-proof door was now unlocked to let Michael out. We walked together in silence to the car and began the fifteen-mile drive back home. I don't think either of us said anything during the entire ride.

Each time the lights of oncoming cars flashed through our windshield, I could see Michael across from me, head down and cheeks damp with moisture.

As the headlights flickered and the little boy sorrowed, these words kept crossing my mind: *Last week we drove home from a science fair; this week from a police station. This one thing remains true: That is still his seat because he is still my son.*

I share this story to illustrate a very important truth about our position as sons and daughters of God. Our Father in heaven regards his children in much the same way earthly parents view their children, only his view is far clearer and his love is far greater. His capacity to love and to care hasn't been damaged by insecurities or fears. He has neither. He is not a dysfunctional parent.

Just as important, his view of his children isn't obscured by their imperfect behavior. His children are *perfect in his eyes.* Paul declares this was God's plan, that through the sacrificial work of Jesus Christ, we would once again be "holy and blameless in his sight" (Ephesians 1:4b). He sees us as holy.

"How can this be?" you might ask. "I don't *act* holy, how can I *be* holy?"

The answer, again, is in our sonship. The holy nature and redemptive work of Jesus Christ has, amazingly, made us new, holy beings! When we receive the Spirit of sonship through the humble, child-like submission of our dependency upon the Father, we are restored back to our dignified positions as sons and daughters of God, just as in the case of the prodigal son. Like the prodigal, we are restored to our original righteous stature as God's children.

Becoming a Christian means leaving a stature of guilt or shame and moving into a stature of innocence. Paul reminds the Colossian believers of this when he says the Father "has *qualified you to share in the inheritance of saints*" and "reconciled you ... *to present you holy in his sight, without blemish and free from accusation*" (Colossians 1:12, 22).

Now, this is very important. Few Christians understand that there are different meanings for the word *holy* when used in its various places in Scripture. For our purposes here, it's essential we understand there is a difference between the *state of holiness*, which I call "being" holiness, and the *conduct of holiness*, which I call "doing" holiness. When we are born again in the Spirit of sonship, we enter into a new state of "being" holiness.

And here's the important point: Although we are not yet perfect in our "doing" holiness, nonetheless, because of the Spirit of sonship, we *are* (right now!) perfect in our "being" holiness. In other words, though we may not be perfect in all our actions, as Christians we have been positioned as the Father's royal sons and daughters. We are bonded to him and we are "holy and blameless in his sight." Now *that's* an amazing thing.

In 2 Corinthians 5:17, Paul announces, "If anyone is in Christ, he is a new creation; the old has gone, the new has come!" Because of Christ, we are *new beings!* The old beings with their old statures are no more! Specifically, these new beings are God's own *sons* and *daughters*. I really like what Christian lecturer David Pawson once said: "We are no longer just homo sapiens, we are *homo novas!* We are like newborn stars!" This is exactly what Paul told the Christians in Philippi when he wrote that we could become "children of God" who "shine like stars in the universe" (Philippians 2:15). Sounds like a promise given to Abraham, doesn't it?

Look at this verse with me in Romans 8:30: "Those he justified (his sons and daughters), he also glorified." Glorified? Isn't *glorified* a term reserved only for God? According to this verse and others, it's also a word used to describe a radical human transformation into a stature of great honor. Amazing! The Father glorifies his children!

Now, if you'll permit me to repeat myself *again*, pretend you've never heard anything like this before, and I hope you hear it in your heart: Those who have been born spiritually through the completed work of Christ are, literally and absolutely, bona fide, *perfectly-*accepted *sons and daughters of God*.

And then, think about this: The Bible calls him King! If you are a Christian woman, then you are a daughter of the King, and that makes you … *a princess!* If you are a Christian man, then you are son of the King. That makes you … *a prince!* You are royalty, and you are incredibly significant. It doesn't get more significant than this. As royal sons and daughters, with our new stature in the Spirit of sonship, we are *perfect in his eyes*.

And finally, we must understand this: The Father would no more terminate his relationship with his children based on an imperfect performance than I would have turned my back on Michael; and our Father in heaven is a million times more just, loving, and merciful than I ever could hope to be.

We are his holy sons and daughters!

And to those who are still contemplating Christianity from the outside, I'm going to say it again: This forgiving Father I have been talking about loves you more than you could ever dream. *That* is the truth!

Chapter 9

Perfect and In Process

*By one sacrifice he has made perfect forever those who are
being made holy.*
— Hebrews 10:14

For the many Christians who struggle with some degree of unhealthy self-concept, I don't believe I can overemphasize the issue of our new and "perfect" stature as the Father's sons and daughters. The Father views us as his own children. We are permanent family members in his royal house — residents of his palace, if you will. We wear the royal robe, the family ring with the royal signet, and, in his eyes, we are and forever will be royally perfect.

Hebrews 10:14 is really important. Here, the author describes the result and on-going effect of Christ's ultimate sacrifice: "By one sacrifice *he has made perfect forever* (past tense) *those who are being made holy* (present tense)."

These next words are excerpted from 2 Corinthians 3:16-18, an almost uncanny text of Scripture: "Whenever anyone turns to the

Lord … there is freedom … we, who … all reflect the Lord's glory, are being transformed (present tense) into his likeness with *ever increasing glory.*" The *glory* continues to increase.

While we are at present "holy in his sight" and "reflecting his glory," we are simultaneously a work in progress. As the Father's children, we are presently "perfect" and, at the same time, in the process of becoming more so! And the glory we've been given is ever-increasing. To use a theological term, we're in the process of sanctification. In other words, we're good and we're getting better.

To illustrate how this works, I need to go back into the realm of memories. This memory begins in San Pedro, California, where both Kathy and I were raised and where we lived during our first few years of marriage.

It actually starts April 30, 1968, the day that jolly nurse led me down the hall and into the delivery room to see my wife and newborn baby. As I said before, I will never forget how I felt when I held our baby girl in my arms for the very first time. I was dazed with love. This little child I called my own was absolutely perfect.

"Honey, she's perrrrfect," I said. Kathy smiled wide and teary.

Still holding Michelle in my arms, I turned to the doctor — who, by the way, was a man nearing retirement and who had no doubt already delivered a bajillion babies — and inquired, "Isn't she the most beautiful and perfect baby you've ever seen?"

He glanced up at me over the top of the half-moon reading glasses resting low on his nose. Then, returning his attention to the medical chart in hand, he replied in an aging, upward slide, "Uhummmmm."

"Seriously, doctor? She's really the most beautiful and perfect baby you've *ever seen?*"

"Uhummmmm."

Imagine, even this experienced doctor was certain she was the most beautiful and perfect baby ever.

In retrospect, what's strange about this is that the word *beautiful* is, admittedly, a peculiar choice of words to use when describing a newborn. In my opinion, all newborn babies appear rather odd and, well … messy. In fact, they are covered with a gooey, unbecoming yellow substance. When I expressed my concern about the visible condition of my little girl, my nurse friend explained to me that this yellow substance was nature's protective lanolin, and every baby comes out that way.

After the explanation, I decided yellow was a fine color. To be honest, if she had been missing an arm or an ear, I know I still would have felt the same way. She was my daughter, and she was perfect.

All of a sudden, my nurse friend took charge and extracted *my* baby girl from my arms, explaining that she needed to clean her up and other nurse-type things.

"You be careful with her now," I ordered.

A few minutes later, one of the attendants wheeled Michelle's little cart over by the viewing window of the hospital nursery so family members could get an introduction. I remember my dad peering over my shoulder to get his first look at his very first grandchild.

"Isn't she beautiful, Dad?"

"She sure is, son."

"Look Dad, her skin is dark olive. Why, she's even better than she was in the delivery room!"

"Uhummm," he responded, sounding much like the doctor.

A few days later, we brought her home from the hospital. Kathy had her dressed in a pretty little pink outfit Grandma had bought for her. I couldn't believe it — she was even more beautiful than she was in the nursery.

I'll never forget getting her ready for church one Sunday. Kathy took the tuft of hair on top of Michelle's head and bunched it together, supporting it with some kind of girlie-bow so it stood straight up in the air, branching open at the top in every direction.

Naturally, I asked, "Kathy, what's that on top of her head?"

"That's her hair," she said.

"It looks like a palm tree," I said.

"It's her hair," she retorted through her teeth while simultaneously smiling at her little princess, "and it looks beautiful."

"Are you *sure* it looks beautiful?" I inquired, now with a little more respect.

"Very sure," she said, lifting the baby, complete with new hairdo, up into her arms.

"It does make her look … taller too," I responded.

A couple of hours later, after church was over and people were doing their weekly catching up in the back of the sanctuary, a half-dozen or so ladies circled Kathy and our little girl. At the same time, about the same number of us men formed a circle right next to the ladies to do our man talk.

I pretended to be listening to the man talk, but I couldn't help overhearing the ladies.

"Isn't her hair darling?" one of the ladies asked.

"Oh my, yes!" said the others.

One of the men happened to notice my head turned slightly in the direction of the ladies' circle and turned his head to look at the baby.

"What's that on top of her head?" he asked.

"That's her hair," I retorted, "and it looks beautiful!"

He looked once more at my little girl and said, "It looks like a palm tree."

In time, Michelle's hair grew out and the palm tree sort of slid to the back of her head where it hung, quite justified, as a sweet little ponytail. It wasn't long after that Kathy was combing that ponytail one Monday morning for Michelle's first day of kindergarten. Michelle was even prettier than before and smarter too. In no time at all, she was reading and writing all by herself.

Day after day, year after year, she got better and better.

Finally, the day came when I got to walk my little girl down the aisle. It was less than a week after Christmas, and the huge sanctuary was decorated in traditional fashion. I was wearing a black tuxedo, and Michelle was wearing a beautiful white, flowing wedding gown. She was perfect.

As we moved down the aisle, I was bursting with pride. Michelle clung to my arm, and I heard her whisper through her smile, "Daddy, slow down, you're walking too fast."

When we came to a stop, I kissed my daughter's olive cheeks and then moved forward toward the altar from where I had the privilege of performing the wedding ceremony.

About halfway through the service, I came to the part where I was supposed to exhort the bride and groom. When I looked at Michelle, I completely lost my train of thought, distracted by her beautiful, dark brown eyes. Through her veil, she just stared, innocent and loving, deep into my eyes. I stared back.

"Michelle," I said in a weak and cracking voice, "Michelle, it's the time in the ceremony to exhort you ... but I can't think of anything to exhort you about. I can't remember anything you've ever done ... wrong."

Right there we began to lose it. Michelle's eyes filled with tears. Her sister, the maid of honor, started wiping tears from her eyes. Mom, in the front row, began to do the same, and I ... I just choked up.

We made it through, but in those moments, as I stared at Michelle, my mind wandered back to the first time I saw her in the hospital delivery room. I thought, *She was perfect then in yellow ... she is even more perfect now in white.*

——

The message? Though none of us have been perfect in behavior, we who are God's children are in a holy process, and "perfect" is how the Father sees us. Move over unhealthy self-worth! We are perfect in his eyes, and we're in the process of getting better.

Chapter 10

The Things That Shape Us

The one who trusts in Him will never be put to shame.
— Romans 9:33

———

His name, let's say, was Steven. He was a thirty-four-year-old Christian man living in Southern California. He could have been nine, sixteen, forty-three, or eighty-five. He could just as easily have been a woman, for that matter; single, married, divorced, or widowed. He could have been from Japan, Bolivia, or Latvia. I've met with many just like Steven, men and women of various backgrounds from six continents who could identify with Steven's problem: an internal, ongoing struggle with the kind of person he thought he was.

It was at the end of a three-day seminar in which I had been speaking on the subject of the Father and his children. Following the last evening session, I allowed for a response and application time for any who wanted to stay around awhile, talk, and pray. As often happened after these final sessions, the majority ended up staying for more than an hour, almost all of them, in their own way, sincerely reaching out, not just to their God, but to their *Father*.

While moving through the crowd, listening to the voluntary and genuine statements, prayers, and commitments of many dear folks, I saw Steven. He had been sitting alone, quietly weeping for some time. I sat down beside him and asked if he would like some support. He nodded. Then, after telling me his name, he leaned over, elbows on his knees and head in his hands, and began to sob. After a minute or more, with deep and tearful emotions, he stuttered out words I've heard a lot of times before: "I can't believe ... God ... could ever ... forgive ... *me*." I paused a few moments and then asked, "And why, Steven, do you think he could never forgive you?" After another minute of waiting, he looked at me and sobbed through these words: "I told ... God ... 'F--- *you* God!'"

Steven shook and cried uncontrollably. I put my arm around his shoulders and said, "Steven, I want to tell you two things. First of all, your Father in heaven has a pretty strong and healthy self-concept. He doesn't fall apart if someone says 'F--- you' to him. If *I* ever heard that from one of my children, I could handle it and would certainly be able to forgive them — and *I* am an imperfect earth dad! So give your ultimate, *perfect* Father some credit here, and trust in his *better* ability, nature, and desire to forgive *you*.

"Second, the Bible says whatever is forgiven on earth, by his authority, is forgiven in heaven. Steven, on his behalf and by his authority, I tell you, you are forgiven. The Father forgives you, Steven, and that's that. Oh, and he wants you to know you're his son and he loves you more than you could ever know."

Staring at me for several seconds with big, teary, hopeful eyes, he asked: "He loves *me* that much?"

"Yep, Steven, he loves *you* that much."

"I never knew before; I never knew."

———

Why is it even many Christians who have been "re-birthed" as the Father's sons and daughters still don't feel fully okay and fully loved? We read that "God so loves us" and sees us as holy and blameless in his eyes — even glorified — yet huge numbers still struggle with an uneasy uncertainness about it all. Why do these *spiritual* people continue harboring unhealthy self concepts, like exaggerated ego, unworthiness, subtle or even full-on shame?

First, let's take a step back and ask how this stuff gets into us in the first place. To repeat what Bradshaw said: "The only way a child has of developing a sense of self is through relationship with another…. We can only know ourselves in the mirroring eyes of our primary caregivers." Based on this, I believe an unhealthy sense of self is many times planted on the inside, through no fault of our own, during our early developing years. It happens through relationship (mutuality) with *imperfect* caregivers. If their "mirroring" eyes sent painful or shaming messages, we assumed those messages to be true. Plain and simple, the majority of humans have an unhealthy view of themselves because of the harmful vibes, or worse, which they received from their dad or mom or other caregivers.

Parents are supposed to love and honor their children. They are given the honorable assignment of validating their children on behalf of God the Father. The parents' mission statement should emphasize the words: We will make our kids feel *valuable*. Daily parental actions should be filled with affection, teaching, goal setting, quality feed-back, affirmation, guidance, and all those important things children need in order to grow up with a strong sense of significance, well-being, and purpose.

But, if parents are still dealing with unhealthy self concepts themselves, then most often the children of these parents end up feeling neglected and essentially on their own. They store up their caregivers' painful, sometimes shaming messages, which, when added up, eventually serve to define them as being insignificant.

Steven was, apparently, one who had been dealing with shame. He felt guilty for cursing God, and rightly so, but it was his ownership of shame that caused him to think he had done the unforgivable.

Steven "saw," though, and seemed to be freed. I felt the "strings" were cut as he prayed one of the most profound prayers I had ever heard. It was from deep inside, and it was powerful.

I didn't have the chance to talk further with Steven, so I didn't learn anything about his past or the reasons for his sad self view — but there were reasons. What I do know is he met happiness that night in California. He met his heavenly Father.

As I said, I've talked with many men and women from different countries and walks of life. I learned early on in my teaching venues that pain, shame, hurt — none of these discriminate against one human kind over another. There are lots of stories I could share. One that comes to me at the moment is of a godly, elderly man I met while speaking years ago at the Youth With A Mission (YWAM) University of the Nations' campus in Kona, Hawaii.

It was at the end of a week of teaching on the subject of son- and daughtership to a group of maybe a hundred Christian leaders from a number of different nations. Once again, during a response and application time, I began to walk around the room, supporting those who were praying and voicing their deep feelings to their heavenly Father. After ten minutes or so I heard someone *wailing*. A few of the class leaders and I moved toward an older man who was expressing serious grief from way down inside.

After at least a minute or more, I remember hearing this gentleman of eighty-plus years sob out in a most tearful and broken way: "Father in heaven, please forgive me for transferring blame onto *you*. I have felt so hurt all these years. My dad ... he promised ... to take ... me fishing ... and ... he never did."

Broken promises, given in a decade long gone by, from a care-giver who didn't care enough. And now, a young boy in weathered, old-man skin finally finds a validating Father he can trust.

———

As with Steven, I don't know what things had shaped the gentleman I met in Kona. I do know a lot about how I was shaped.

Before I share a little about my shaping as a boy, I feel it's important to say this: In thinking or talking about one's parents, it's very important to keep things in the right perspective. In the letter to the Ephesians, right after Paul talks about properly relating to parents and other earthly authorities, he reminds us that "our struggle is not against flesh and blood, but ... against the spiritual forces of evil in the heavenly realms" (Ephesians 6:12). In other words, there's a more powerful activity going on out there than just human, flesh-and-blood activity, and this thing can play a huge role in our life development.

Paul is essentially saying it's the "forces of evil in the heavenly realms" that are the real source of our problems. These dark powers come against the children, "pulling the puppet strings" and passing down destructive messages from one generation to the next. It should be at *these powers* we focus our attack — not at earthly caregivers.

Let us always remember that our caregivers were recipients of harmful messages long before we were, and in many cases, their pain was even greater than ours. It's non-productive and self-destructive to hold judgments against them or anyone. Plus, Jesus commands us *not* to judge. Instead of judgment, we need to remember we are God's children now. Because we're his sons and daughters, we should begin to think with grace, profit from what we've learned, and keep strengthening our own caregiving skills.

———

I loved my mom and dad and they loved me. But I saw firsthand how harmful messages invaded their lives.

My mom must have been the sweetest little girl growing up because she was such a dear, sweet mother. But she was shamed by a very harsh father, my grandfather. As a young boy growing up, I witnessed his habit of belittling or lashing out at his fearful little wife, my grandma, and at his three children, mostly my mom. She grew up in fear.

When I was eighteen years old, I drove my mom one summer day to visit Grandpa, who was on his death bed in a Los Angeles hospital. I remember as if it were yesterday how coldly he acted. Only minutes after we arrived, he ripped into my mom with everything he had left; calling her every demeaning thing he could think of. His voice continued to rise until my mom finally broke and began sobbing. Her pain was horrible to watch.

With my mouth open in shock, I put my arms around her as she slumped, both hands covering her face, into a low posture of pain and shame. I stared at the angry old man on the bed whom, oddly enough, I had loved as well as feared. I couldn't stand it any longer. With a trembling voice, I somehow managed to say, "My mom is one of the most wonderful women in the world. Don't you EVER talk to her that way AGAIN!" Tearful now and shaking even more, I lifted her cowering frame more upright, turned her away from his bedside, and helped walk my trembling mother — reduced to a little girl — out of the hospital. The ride home was sorrowful.

We never saw Grandpa alive again.

My mom has always has been a completely dedicated Christian woman. She has lived with deep spiritual convictions all her life. But the scars of shame delivered by her father and the fear imprinted by her fearful mother have lingered on now for 87 years. Some of both had been passed down to me.

My dad was a high achiever. He graduated second in officer's training school and flew as a Navy pilot during World War II. He later became a mechanical engineer, then chief engineer, and, in time, a company vice president with nearly thirty patents to his name. He told me more than once he had read over a thousand books before his twenty-first birthday. By the time I was twenty-one, I had read two, plus or minus.

Being right brained and somewhat ADD kept me on an opposite page from Dad. I liked sports and music. He liked math and science. He wanted me to become a doctor, an astronomer, or an officer after I fulfilled his dream for me of graduating from the Annapolis Naval Academy. My dream job was to be a stubble-bearded western movie hero with a short, thin, unlit cigar always clenched between my teeth. Our communication often amounted to Dad saying things like, "Did you finish your yard work?" or "What's this with your report card?" He wasn't generally pleased with my answers. If he was, he didn't show it.

I don't remember ever getting affection from Dad. Every night when he got home from work, my mom would faithfully greet him at the front door with a big hug and kiss. As I recall, he would then put his arms around each of my three younger sisters — but never me. I sort of chalked it up to the don't-hug-the-son rule; the "man thing." I never knew my dad's father, as he died when I was a toddler, but I would bet a thousand hugs this "rule" was something handed down by Grandpa.

Feeling like I always disappointed my dad created a lot of self-doubt about myself and my future. Couple that with the fear modeled by my otherwise good and loving mother, and there you have it — me.

I was a young person like so many others: destined to feel like a failure, living with unreasonable worry, and on track toward panic.

———

I've said children can store up harmful messages. Some are messages of *rejection*. Some forms of rejection are easy to identify, but others, though damaging, are not so clear. They've become somewhat of a blur in the maze of memories.

Charles Solomon, author of the book *The Ins and Outs of Rejection*, defines two kinds of rejection that can be imposed on children by their primary caregivers. The first he calls "overt" rejection; that which is harsh and obvious. Examples of overt rejection are physical abandonment (intentional or as the result of divorce), and physical, sexual, or mental abuse.

The second kind of rejection Solomon refers to as "covert" rejection. This kind of rejection is far more common yet far less conspicuous as a culprit. The following are some of Solomon's examples of covert rejection. Maybe one or more of these will stand out to you; some did to me.

Covert rejection can be experienced when a caregiver:

- manifests inconsistent behavior and emotion
- shows favoritism to a brother or sister
- implies the child is the wrong sex
- is performance oriented
- has unfair expectations
- has no expectations
- draws comparisons, one child against another
- is too frequently absent
- doesn't show enough interest or attention
- gives too much attention
- doesn't give enough affection
- overprotects
- is rule oriented
- piles on too much responsibility
- doesn't provide enough rules or boundaries
- doesn't give enough feedback

- gives too much feedback
- uses unwise choice of words or expressions
- is inconsistent with discipline
- disciplines improperly
- never disciplines
- gives too much freedom
- demands perfection
- doesn't offer enough explanation
- engages in role reversal
- dies prematurely

And you name it. Maybe you can think of something to add to the list.

To paraphrase Solomon, the consequences of covert rejection can be just as bad as those of overt rejection, and all the result of false messages.

Children who have been the victims of rejection of any kind can easily end up feeling alone, insignificant, and insecure. Some get stuck in the "worm syndrome" and act out their days accordingly. Many spend their lives struggling to overcome their unhappy identity by trying to prove something or achieve perfection. Others strive to become someone else. A number go into hiding. Family heroes or scapegoats, ultra independents or co-dependents, whatever kind of unhealthy self shows up, it's always that — unhealthy.

What's the answer to the unhealthy self? It's this: The most loving caregiver of all wants to help us make a clean break from every one of those harmful messages that shaped us so he can reshape us the *right* way.

In the first chapter, I shared about my emotional unraveling, and in the following chapters, I'll show the strange way in which the answers came — real solutions straight from heaven. No matter where you are spiritually, I believe the heavenly Father has something new and wonderful ahead just for you.

PART FOUR
A Remarkable Recovery

Strange as it will sound,
this is what happened to me.

Chapter 11

Encounter in the Desert

*Oh God, you are my God, earnestly I seek you; my soul
thirsts for you, my body longs for you, in a dry and weary
land where there is no water.*
— Psalm 63:1

⸻

*T*he days and nights following my first panic attack were the
most difficult of my life. From one moment to the next, I was
anxiety's plaything. When you become a victim of fear, an
otherwise normal day turns into an endless nightmare, and the
resulting confusion distorts everything — people, places, events. In a
heartbeat, the smallest incident becomes a gigantic hurdle to
surmount. Before I could deal with one obstacle, a new giant would
appear out of nowhere. A victim of fear and confusion creates his or
her own giants out of nothing. In fact, the majority of my "giant" problems were self-made. Time was distorted too. It's difficult to explain,
but sometimes I wasn't sure if I was living in the past, the present, or

somewhere in the future. Anxiety is incredibly disorienting and destructive.

If there is one favorite companion of fear, it would be loneliness. Even though I was surrounded by supportive family and friends, I still felt desperately alone and isolated in my abnormal psychological condition. Although my loved ones tried to relate to my situation, they simply could not identify with my experience. I felt I was going crazy ... all by myself! The combination of fear, loneliness, and craziness made me even more frantic. When you are trapped in the cage of your own mind, you're desperate to escape. I didn't want to die — I was far too afraid of that scenario — but I didn't want to live in this constant state of anxiety either. Imagining my life as an unending series of panic attacks scared me senseless, *driving* me to seek some avenue of escape.

I began a regimented, healthy diet; consumed assorted vitamins by the hundreds, and visited several doctors. The doctors offered no useful course of treatment, but rather, the reverse — they insinuated my mental condition was even worse than I thought. The only clear advice they offered was to exercise. So I did. I ran and ran and ran and ran, but it brought little relief except that exhaustion temporarily replaced the fear.

In my own anxious way, I tried the most obvious course for a so-called "spiritual man" to pursue. I asked God about my situation. No, I *begged* God night and day to help me. It's interesting how desperation can get you to want God's help. But begging God didn't seem to help either. I felt guilty for begging, guilty for being like this. My faith in prayer was meager at best. Besides, asking God for help seemed a little selfish and a little late in coming. This horrific fear was undermining my whole spiritual being. I felt weak and sometimes pitiful. My friends really couldn't help me (or maybe I wasn't listening), and I didn't feel I deserved God's help. So I ran, partly in an effort to oppose the anxiety, and in retrospect, I suspect in an effort to punish myself for my "badness" and discipline myself into some "betterness."

One of my routine runs was located north of our subdivision down a long, beautiful country road. I enjoyed the feeling of leaving civilization behind me. The only thing I didn't like about this particular stretch of highway was the unfriendly presence of a small, unmanaged cemetery, which lingered, menacing, along the roadside about a mile from our home. Every day it seemed to call my name as I crossed to the opposite side of the road, not daring to look or listen.

As I neared the cemetery on this particular day, I felt even more anxious than usual. My emotional distress was further compounded by a jittery, caffeine-like agitation in my head and chest. I turned off the pavement, pushed my feet through the tall grass of the barrow pit, sat down on the embankment, and gazed at the western slopes of the Continental Divide.

Sitting there, alone and staring, a most unusual event occurred, one I can only describe as a vision. Though my body never left Montana, my mind somehow traveled to a far off place. I wasn't accustomed to or inclined toward such supernatural phenomena, but this experience was so real, it was as if I had actually been transported. I didn't know it then, but this strange experience would become the greatest turning point in my life.

The mountain scene in front of me disappeared. I found myself lying face down in a desert, isolated and pinned to the earth by a heavy weight of sorrow and trepidation. It took effort to lift my head. My sweat-drenched face was bearded with sand, which I spat from my mouth as I stared at a vast, scorching desert. No sign of life, former or present; just white, flat stretches of sand as far as the eye could see. A watery mirage of desert thermals wavered in the distance.

This place scared me and I wanted out.

The blistering sun was fixed in a stationary position directly overhead, making it impossible in the flat terrain to discern north from south or east from west. I turned my head, trying to see where I had come from, but there were no tracks. How did I get here? Where was I now? Where should I go?

But I couldn't go; I couldn't move. My arms and legs were numb and my strength was gone. I was absolutely alone; lost and dying in a desert of obscurity. I couldn't even remember my name. This empty, lifeless desert epitomized my innermost feelings. My fear became more intense.

After what seemed like hours of staring helplessly into the distance, I saw something new. A small, bright, shining object appeared on the horizon before me. It looked as if someone was trying to send a signal of some kind, as if someone was flashing a mirror at me. As the flashing grew brighter, I realized it was coming from a horse carrying a rider. Soon I could see it was an enormous white horse; its rider was some kind of soldier. The soldier wore a white head covering with a long veil that flowed behind him as his mighty horse powered toward me. He wore a silver breastplate that burned brilliantly in the sun — it hurt my eyes. The stallion, too, radiated; its bridle and saddle decorated with silver and jewels. The equestrian pair was magnificent — and terrifying. The thought struck me: This was the angel of death coming for me!

Death — my greatest fear. I had convinced myself from the moment of my first panic attack that my true problem was medical, a bad heart. Perhaps this was the moment, I thought, as the horse and rider closed the distance, when death would grab me. I whimpered in terror as I struggled to move, but without an inch of success. I buried my face in the sand, hoping when I lifted it again they would be gone.

But when I raised my head, the horse and rider came closer still. Now a few hundred yards from me, I could hear the heavy breathing of the charging steed. A hundred yards ... fifty ... death was closing in on me at a supernatural speed. I groaned and buried my face in the sand once more. Within seconds, the white stallion slid to a complete stop in front of me, spraying sand over the back and length of my body.

I could feel the animal's hot, threatening breath on the back of my neck. Turning my head slightly, I opened one eye to see the shadow thrown by the great horse as it rose high in the air on its hind legs. I could also see the shadow of the soldier as he lifted his sword triumphantly to the sun. I was certain that when the horse came down my life would be over. I trembled, waiting.

The horse came down with a tremendous thud. I tightened my body with every ounce of remaining energy and braced myself for the soldier's blade.

Quiet. For a minute or more I lay there shaking. Nothing happened. More quiet.

After more than a minute, I slowly raised my head in hopes of ending the agony of waiting and uncertainty. I jerked away at the sight of an object pointed right at me some six inches away from my face. At second glance, I was surprised to find it was not a sword after all. The soldier, leaning down from his saddle, was extending a scrolled, parchment-like document secured by a small gold ribbon.

Studying the situation, I finally decided the soldier was offering it to me. Still trembling, I managed to lift my right hand high enough to grasp the scroll. But strangely, he wouldn't let go of it. Confused by his response, I looked up at him in search of some explanation. I was shocked by what I saw. The veil had fallen from his face. The rider on the horse was *me! Except he was the "me" I longed to be!*

The rider embodied confidence. His jaw was set, indicating his fearlessness and strength. He was a man under control, whose eyes expressed both passion and power. His countenance portrayed tremendous authority and complete peace. This soldier knew exactly who he was and where he had come from. I glanced behind his horse to see the tracks in the sand. Now, upon completion of a mission, he knew exactly where he would be going. He was awesome; I would never forget him. *I knew he was a prince.* The only question that came to mind, shouted out with sorrow from deep inside me, was: *Why can't I be him?*

It was at that precise moment I heard a powerful voice break through the white-hot skies and say: *"Today is your day. In your hand, you hold your birthright."*

I gasped, and tears began to course down my sweaty face. Then I realized the rider had released the scroll. I stared at the parchment clutched in my shaking hand with just a hint of understanding. With my mouth open in amazement, I looked up again for answers — but the horse and rider had vanished.

I bolted to my feet as the Rocky Mountains of Montana broke into view. "Come back," I yelled. "Come back!"

Chapter 12

The City of the King

They are led in with joy and gladness; they enter the palace of the king.
— Psalm 45:15

———

*A*fter the vision faded, I ran home as fast as I could. I couldn't believe what had happened. Elated, yet frustrated, I cried, "But God, the vision, what's the meaning? I need to know the meaning!"

As I drew closer to home, I realized it was senseless to hurry. Although I wanted to share my experience with Kathy, I began to question its reality and validity. Perhaps it was all my imagination, or I only wanted the vision to have significance. So I decided to remain silent through the remainder of the day. Late into the night, I internally repeated my anxious question, *What does it all mean?* Finally, I fell asleep about midnight, but sometime toward morning, I had a dream; one I will never, ever forget.

In this dream, it was *me — David!* — riding across the desert on a white horse. The experience was new and incredible, yet as familiar as if I had ridden this animal for ten thousand years. The horse knew me well; I was his master and friend.

We galloped for many miles and countless hours across the desert floor. The gallant steed never tired as he charged for home, retracing the tracks he had pounded into the sands earlier that day. I had completed a mission, and I rode with dignity and unshakable joy.

Near day's end, we ascended a huge dune, and as we crested its top and lunged down its backside, I beheld an enormous and magnificent city surrounded by a massive wall stretching out of sight in both directions.

The charger headed for the main gate, the entrance to the most magnificent palace imaginable towering over the city. No such palace ever existed in any earthly kingdom. It stood out like a gigantic redwood in a field of wheat.

Three angels guarding the gate awaited my return. I rode toward them, jumping from the saddle as my horse came to an abrupt stop. The captain of the guard, a striking, powerful creature, approached me and took the reins of my horse. He gazed at me with respect and asked, "How did it go today, Sir David?" Although part of me was astonished by this designation of nobility, I replied with poise, "It went well, thank you."

The other two guardsmen pushed open the gates as I stepped through the great passageway. They followed me and the captain, who was now leading my horse. We entered a vast sandy courtyard bordering the front and sides of the immense palace. Inside the courtyard, hundreds of groups of people had gathered together in an orderly fashion to perform different creative exercises. The whole scene was amazing and extremely satisfying to watch. There were artists producing a variety of crafts and magnificent paintings; dancers with marvelous style and grace; musicians performing the most beautiful music; writers inventing fascinating stories; engineers developing new and unusual inventions. Orators and audiences, practitioners and observers: all learning, creating, performing, and living life to the fullest — as it was meant to be.

One particular group caught my attention. A dozen young men and women were actively drilling in some martial art form. Each held

THE CITY OF THE KING   97

a sword, which they flashed and swirled in perfect harmony. In the middle of the exercise, one of the young brothers awkwardly dropped his sword at his side. As the oldest brother in a family with three younger sisters, I had, unfortunately, developed a habit of teasing, which, for a moment, tempted me to make some clever remark to this young brother. But the "new" side of me declined to resort to my old habit. Instead, I began to view this boy with honor, as a growing young warrior. At that precise moment, an older brother standing nearby knelt in the sand, lifted the sword, and respectfully presented it to his young comrade. With gratitude, the younger brother took the sword and moved back into the ranks.

Then I heard the Father's voice saying, "In the kingdom of heaven, there is no competition." Now, as a person who loves sports and games, I didn't then and don't now believe this statement meant God condemns athletic or other healthy activities. Healthy competition will surely go on forever. What I understood the Father to mean was, in the kingdom, no one has to, and no one will ever have to compete to *establish* his or her significance. No one will ever have to fight to *keep* significance. There will never be an activity in the Father's house that will intrude upon the integrity of even *one* of his children.

From the outer courtyard, I climbed the steps to the west entrance of the palace where I entered a vast hallway nearly a hundred yards long. As I began to walk down the corridor, I noticed an open door on my left. Stopping for a moment, I saw that the door opened into a room filled with dozens of my sisters preparing themselves for some grand occasion. They brushed one another's hair and helped each other with makeup. As I observed their beauty and grace, I was overwhelmed with a sense of devotion and honor for them. Two words seemed to visually drift toward the doorway: dignity and beauty.

One of the girls having her hair braided spotted me and turned to raise her right hand in welcome, calling my name, "David!" At once, the roomful of sisters joined in her sincere greeting. I felt such affection and respect coming from all of them. With my hands at my side, I bowed with respect, then raised my right hand in a parting salute and continued down the hallway.

At the end of this lengthy corridor, I came to a huge pair of raised-panel doors nearly as tall and wide as the hallway itself. I pushed them open to reveal a massive dining hall containing a table of immense proportions beginning some fifty feet to my left and continuing beyond my range of vision to the right. On both sides of the table, as far as the eye could see, countless brothers and sisters were enjoying a beautiful evening meal together in what struck me as the most harmonious sense of family I could imagine.

After closing the doors, I turned to locate my empty seat, which was a little to my right about twenty-five seats from the head of the table. As I approached my place, I noticed out of the corner of my eye that the person at the head of the table rose from his seat, pushed back his chair, and walked across the room until he stood directly in my path.

In a most tender way, he stretched out his arms toward me and placed his strong hands lovingly on each of my shoulders. With an intense look of pride and compassion, he looked into my eyes and greeted me with words similar to those of the angel's at the gate. Yet these few simple words were far more profound. These words penetrated my soul and changed my life forever. He said, "How did it go today, *my son?*"

I woke up … and I *woke* up. Tears streamed down my face as this new revelation opened my eyes to the rest of my life. I didn't wake up a sales manager, seminar speaker, or pastor. I didn't wake up a husband, father, or spiritual leader.

I woke up … a SON!

I got up. I got dressed. I walked downstairs, and I began my life.

Chapter 13

The Great Transition

*So he got up and went to his father. But while he was still a
long way off, his father saw him and was filled with compassion for him; he ran to his son, threw his arms around him
and kissed him.*
— Luke 15:20

———

A vision of a desert and a dream of a palace started me down the
path of an incredible transition. And while I have other
personal stories and unusual events to share with you from my
journey, before you read much farther, I want to say this particular
chapter may well prove to be the most important for you. You might
want to bookmark it to revisit.

If the concept of the Spirit of sonship is registering with you,
and if you desire to move from where you *are* into the place where you
confidently know your position as one of the Father's children, then
the next step is to take action. Here is your opportunity. I'd like to
suggest some things you can do to help you begin your own transition.

Keep in mind you are embracing what has been the Father's only objective throughout history — to have his sons and daughters back.

Not all of these responses may be applicable in your situation, and there may be others not listed here that come to your mind. Pray and ask the Father in heaven to help you to know what applies and how you should personally and specifically respond. I hope you are starting to understand that he loves you more than you ever thought, and he wants to give you his best. He longs for you to experience ultimate mutuality with him.

The walk home is not that much longer.

———

As you begin your own transition, first remember that living in the Spirit of sonship is only made possible by the sacrificial life and death of Jesus Christ, the one called Emmanuel, God with us. Sent from heaven and living in perfect relationship, or mutuality, with God, Jesus became our substitute and paid the price for the consequences of our broken relationship with the Father. Because of his actions on our behalf, this first Son has given you and me the right to become the Father's children once again. As we read in John 1:12: "To all who received him (Jesus Christ), to those who believed in his name, he gave the right to become children of God."

Our journey out of a stained and earthly self-concept into a new position of true honor and significance starts at the time when we make the decision to "believe and receive" Jesus. Remember again the words Jesus spoke to Nicodemus in John 3:5-7, where he said, "I tell you the truth, no one can enter the kingdom of God unless he is born of … the Spirit … the Spirit gives birth to spirit … 'You must be born again.'"

So, if you haven't already done so, I urge you to do the following:

1. Receive Jesus, the great Lord, the great Christ of Scriptures. State your belief in him, and let the Spirit he speaks of give birth to a brand new you!

Talk to him. Speak out loud so you can hear yourself. If you're not sure what to say, I'd like to help you with the words:

Lord, please forgive me for living my life independent of you. Forgive me for the sinful choices I made along the way. Today, I'm making the choice to follow you — I'm following you home. I really do believe you, Lord, and I receive you. And I ask, right now, for your Spirit to give birth to a new spirit inside me, to birth a new me. I ask to be born a second time, this time as a child of the heavenly Father.

If that sounds too simple, think on this: the Father, the Son, and the Spirit — the most loving, holy beings with the most exceptional of all minds — did the hard and complicated things to make it that easy and simple.

If you prayed that prayer, something powerful just happened. You are a *new you!* It would be a very good thing to pause here just to thank him.

2. Ask God — *your* Father in heaven — for forgiveness of any misjudgments, mistrust, or anger you have held against him.

Many people, both inside and outside of Christianity, harbor negative judgments against God, sometimes subconsciously, thinking he is to blame for all their bad experiences. In reality, it is mostly human choices that have created suffering. God gave man freedom of choice, which is what makes humans such significant beings. As a consequence, God is not free to interrupt all the choices of man, or he would end up *destroying* man's freedom and significance. Instead, God's strategy has been to secure an abundant inheritance for his children by means of his remarkable, sacrificial plan, all the while keeping man's freedom of choice and significance intact.

You can be sure, however, our Father gets angry when someone violates another human being. There are copious Scriptures that give clear evidence of the strong emotional response of God when someone brings evil on another, and, sooner or later, the violator will suffer consequences for evil choices.

And while some people continue to choose evil, the Father in heaven weeps for the victims and moves toward them with a motive of rescuing love. You can also be sure, whether on earth or in heaven, the Father *will* demonstrate his care, compassion, power, and justice for every victim that has ever lived. If only the victims would come to understand the Father is one hundred percent on their side.

Perhaps you realize now you've held unwarranted feelings of mistrust toward the heavenly Father, feelings that have prevented you from even wanting to be his child. If this is the case, you can experience real freedom from these feelings by asking his forgiveness. In your own words, your prayer could start something like this: *"Father, please forgive me for my mistrust in you ..."* You'll know what else to say. After you've spoken, he comes close to forgive and comfort. That's what a good father does.

3. If you've been a Christian for some time, and if the following applies to you, ask your Father to forgive *you* for continuing to live in an ongoing "spirit of independence."

If you have continued to move in a spirit of independence, saying, "I can do it on my own," then God's gift of repentance can turn things around for you. Ask your Father in heaven to forgive you for your independent spirit, offering to be completely dependent upon him from now on. It's amazing how your perspective will change when you take this genuine action. So, *"Father, forgive me ..."*

4. On the other hand, if the following applies, ask your Father to forgive you for any improper or misplaced dependency upon others, and then verbalize your trust in and dependency upon him.

For many, the continual need to be approved, or validated, by earthly caregivers, whether past or present, keeps them from experiencing the *Father's* validation.

Make the shift. Quit depending upon others for your significance, and with sincere repentance, volunteer a new dependence upon the perfect and eternal Caregiver. In words something like this, you might say: *"Father, forgive me for putting all my dependency only upon others. On this day, I'm placing my dependency upon you."*

5. If the following applies to you, ask your Father for forgiveness for any anger or bitterness you have held toward any caregivers in your past.

It's destructive to our very identity to be confined in the prison of bitterness, and that's exactly what bitterness is — a prison. Though we may think *we* are in control, we're not. In reality, bitterness has *us* locked up and under *its* control. And we remain prisoners long after our caregivers have moved on.

Forgiveness is the key to the prison door! It may take a while to feel a complete emotional release, but freedom begins by making a choice to forgive. Just as Jesus, by an act of his will, forgave those who were crucifying him, so we, by an act of our will, have the power to extend forgiveness. This act of forgiveness, like that of Jesus, is certifiably recognized in heaven. Forgiveness extended by choice is a powerful step toward ultimate freedom and significance.

Jesus said to pray, "Forgive us our trespasses as we forgive those who trespass against us." Pray aloud and let the Father hear you extend forgiveness toward caregivers or any others who have let you down — then feel your *own* forgiveness.

6. Release those former caregivers to the Father, and let him take over. Then pray the Father would give them a revelation of the Spirit of sonship, that they would be released from their own hurt, insecurity, and shame.

In addition to forgiving, it's important to give those caregivers into the Father's hands. Pray for them; even bless them. As difficult as it may sound to do, like forgiveness, praying for those who have hurt you can bring tremendous healing, not only in that person's life but in your own life as well. "Give and it shall be given unto you" — it's a kingdom principle.

A final note on forgiving and blessing those who have hurt you: For many, the memories of hurt and pain are severe. It would be insensitive of me to imply that these issues are a snap to deal with. For some, it will take more time and more effort. The Father understands our emotions. After all, he made us in his image, and while on earth, his Son, Jesus, identified with the full spectrum of human emotion. He loves us and completely understands why we feel the way we do about our memories. He was there, hurting with us, when the pain was first inflicted. Now he wants the pain to end.

So begin. Choose to forgive and let the Father take over. And while you process this in the realm of your emotions, it is important to keep reminding yourself you wear a robe of glory. You are not a victim! You are a son or daughter of the ultimate Caregiver!

7. If the following applies to you, ask the Father to forgive you for any shortcomings you have had as a caregiver to others.

God wants to forgive you and heal your sorrow over your own mistakes as caregiver. Ask him for forgiveness. Perhaps you still have the opportunity to ask forgiveness from those you've hurt as well. The Father is granting you time to translate what you have learned into the lives of others — even someone new — who could really use your loving caregiving.

8. Now, take claim to the Spirit of sonship. Make a *final* declaration! Speak out words like these: "Father, I am your son!" or "Father, I am your daughter!"

Take the last step home. Embrace his perfect caregiving, leadership, and validation. And begin acting like you *know* you are his son or his daughter. Mark this day and this time, and remember it forever. May this day become a milestone of remembrance influencing all of your future feelings and actions. You might imagine driving a stake in the ground as a testimony of new ground you've claimed. I like to say, "Drive the stake so deep that hell gets the point!"

Now, make that declaration! Declare with confidence: "Father in heaven, you are my Father! You are *my* Father!!"

9. Pray that the revelation of your Father and the Spirit of sonship keeps growing in you every day.

Ask the Father, "Father, please keep this revelation alive and growing." He loves to respond to these kinds of prayers. If you have to, repeat your prayer until your emotions "get the point." This is what he always wanted for you: to have a life again.

10. And finally — live!

Live, brothers and sisters; live! It's not too late to live the rest of your life with freedom, honor, joy, peace, and purpose. From now on, choose to live with a new mindset. Live! This is the Father's gift to you!

On a clear and cool fall night in 2000, I turned to look out the window of my dad's bedroom and viewed the last goodbye glow of the Montana evening sunset. After a few moments of pondering, I turned back to once again study the face of my dying father, who lay unconscious and motionless, eyes closed, mouth slightly open, on his side near the edge of his small bed.

Sitting with me in the room were my three sisters: Linda, Christine, and Laura. My Michelle was there next to me as well. My mom and Kathy had left the room momentarily. The five of us who remained were silent as we watched him.

He was a much different man than the one I had known as a boy during those years when I felt I was such a disappointment to him. After Kathy and I were married, Dad became a Christian and began a wonderful spiritual journey. He had made the "great transition" and was a changed man for the rest of his life.

After he retired, he and Mom moved to Montana to be close to us. For nearly eighteen years, Dad and I spent many summer days together on Flathead Lake in his old pontoon boat, fishing for the elusive kokanee salmon; or sitting next to each other in his faithful old golf cart while enjoying our favorite past time, or gathering with family for barbeques and get-togethers. Throughout those times, we shared countless warm conversations, a lot of laughter, sometimes tears — and hugs. We grew to love each other as much as any dad and son could love.

And now was the time we would be parting.

Suddenly, Dad began breathing heavily, and to our surprise, for the first time in three days, he opened his eyes.

I moved my chair in as close as I could. Linda moved to sit on his bed and put her hand softly on his side. Michelle now stood quietly behind me with her hands on my shoulders.

I took hold of his bony hand and we stared into each other's eyes. I couldn't help but wonder what he was thinking. And then my thoughts were that I was so amazed with this dad of mine who was so full of faith. He had battled his cancer with such bravery and integrity … and now, he had won. In those final moments, I leaned forward and, hoping he would understand, I said, "Dad, I'm very proud of you." As he looked with love at me, my dad's last rasping words on earth were: "I … proud … *you.*"

Then he looked up at Michelle and smiled endearingly. After a moment or two, something caught his attention above Michelle's head, and he began gazing up at the ceiling with a look of awe and astonishment on his face. He was as wide eyed as I'd ever seen him. Someone very special had come for him. Then, he took one last breath, closed his eyes — and walked up the stairs to our Father's house.

It occurred to me just now while writing this that the visitor who came to take Dad had waited just long enough to let him speak those last words of validation to me. I now understand that *another* father, the heavenly Father, wanted to remind me of how he felt too.

In thinking of how to close this chapter, I clearly felt the Father tell me to tell you something: Right now, as you take your own personal steps with him down the path of great transition … he is very proud of *you*.

PART FIVE

Principles for Well-Being

For three consecutive mornings,
I met with the Holy Spirit. He would talk;
I would listen and write.
(Are you going to keep reading?)

Chapter 14

The Holy Spirit and the Orange Naugahyde Chair

The Counselor, the Holy Spirit, whom the Father will send in
my name, will teach you all things.... Peace I leave with you;
my peace I give to you.
— John 14:26-27

———

*I*n the morning, only a few days after the vision and dream experience, I drove south down Main Street and turned into the parking lot of our church offices. It was an old home, actually, which had been converted into what we called the Ministry Center, and it was there I had resumed my work as an associate pastor. I had resigned my job as a sales manager, and my dear friend, Hal Curtiss, the church's senior pastor, as well as the other church leaders, graciously invited me to begin stepping back into active pastoral ministry.

I arrived earlier than usual this particular morning and was the first one there to unlock the back door leading into the house's old kitchen. As I removed the key, turned the knob, and pushed open the door, I suddenly had a strange feeling there might be someone else inside. I stopped in the doorway, scanned the kitchen, and peered down the hallway leading from the far side of the kitchen to the ministry offices beyond.

Apprehensive, I crossed the kitchen floor, entered the hallway, and stopped at the first door on the right, the one leading into my office. I paused for a moment before turning the knob and pushing the door open. My little office had once been a tiny bedroom. It measured maybe nine feet by nine feet. My small desk and a three-shelf book case crowded the left wall. Facing the desk, in front of the room's only window, was an ugly, old, saggy orange Naugahyde chair. I had found the old armchair in the attic of a house we had once rented. It was a sorry-looking thing with fuzzy stuff sprouting out at the top ends of each arm. People would come in for counsel and unconsciously pick at the fuzz.

Now get this! *There, in my orange Naugahyde chair, I could see in my mind's eye* (another vision) *the presence of the Holy Spirit.* There he sat; legs crossed, arms and hands resting comfortably on the worn-out arms of the old chair.

I know what you're thinking: *David's really flipped out now.* Bear with me.

I looked at him and he looked at me for what must have been ten or fifteen seconds until I finally said, "Hello." He said, "Hello."

While continuing to stare in bewilderment, I closed the door, worked my way around the desk to my left, and sat down. I stared on. He smiled briefly with a warmth I can't describe. After a moment, he spoke these words, "David, we know the fear you've experienced. The Father sent me to help you."

"He did?" I responded with tearful sheepishness.

"Yes, son, he did. Now, I want you to get out some paper and write down everything I tell you."

I understand if you are skeptical. This may sound strange and unfamiliar, but nonetheless, as with the vision and the dream, this is what really happened. Over the course of three consecutive mornings, we met like this. He would talk. I would listen and write. Sometimes I would ask questions out loud to the fascinating Person in the orange Naugahyde chair.

It was more than just a strange experience. It was wonderful, encouraging, and deeply healing. He would tell me to look up a certain passage of Scripture or direct me to a certain page or chapter in the Bible. All of his counsel was backed with Scripture. It was remarkable how therapeutic the biblical passages were when they came with such specific application. I soon realized the Holy Spirit, sent from the Father, was giving me a personal, biblical life prescription for spiritual and emotional well-being.

I wrote down everything and then condensed it all onto one page, folded it to fit in my wallet, and carried it with me everywhere I went for years afterward. It became my substitute for Valium, which I had learned to carry in fear of any possible emotional challenge. If I was ever out driving in my car somewhere and sensed a hint of oncoming panic, I was quick to pull over to the side of the road, yank out my wallet, and meditate on the principles and Scriptures given me on those three special mornings. And the calm would return.

The principles the Spirit shared with me were rooted in Romans 8. This was the chapter he used to wake me up to the powerful and elemental truth of our son- and daughtership, which is the bottom line of the Gospel. And during these morning meetings, he opened my eyes to many of the innate, wonderful, and unchangeable benefits and privileges we own as his sons and daughters.

In verse five it says: "Those who live according to the sinful nature have their *minds set* on what that nature desires; but those who live in accordance with the Spirit have their *minds set* on what the Spirit desires. The mind of sinful man is death, but the mind controlled by the Spirit is life and peace."

Note, in particular, the words *minds set*. Paul is saying that when we are willfully (with our minds) submitted to the Holy Spirit (sent by the Father) and his principles, we are assured that we will experience life and peace as it should be for every Christian. The key to spiritual and emotional wholeness is, again, dependency. We are given new power to maintain personal peace and emotional control when we make a free-willed decision to be dependent (like a child) upon the Father and his counseling Spirit.

Once we've made the decision to be dependent, all we have to do is *listen*. And that was the first thing the Spirit told me to write down. I call it **Principle Number One**. He said, "David, *listen to the Father and you'll receive his power.*"

You don't have to be Abraham or Moses to hear the voice of God. Like all good fathers — and we're talking about the best one here — *God speaks to all of his children.* He knows how badly we need his information and affirmation. He longs for us to hear his voice. It may sound too simple, but all we need to do to hear God's voice is believe he speaks and then make the decision to listen. It is absolutely that simple. As John 10:27 says, "My sheep listen to my voice; I know them, and they follow me." If you would like to know more about this important subject, I would highly recommend two books: *Is That Really You, God?* by Loren Cunningham, founder of Youth With A Mission, and *Hearing the Voice of God* by Joy Dawson.

The main thing to remember is to keep it simple. The Father speaks to our hearts and minds and we listen. Then, as in the lives of Moses and Abraham, he turns on the power supply.

This is the next Scripture I read: "I lift up my eyes to the hills — where does my help come from? My help comes from the Lord, the Maker of heaven and earth. He will not let your foot slip — he who watches over you will not slumber" (Psalm 121:1-3). Pretty great, isn't it? We direct our attention to the Father, who is always awake, and he will supply us with power (strength) and protection.

Next, I was led to Psalm 57:2-3, which also speaks of the power and protection that becomes our provision when we are focused on the Father: "I cry out to God Most High, to God, who fulfills his purpose for me. He sends from heaven and saves me."

The Father wants to speak reassuring words of love and peace to us. The Spirit passed Psalm 94:18-19 on to me: "When I said, 'My foot is slipping,' your love, O Lord, supported me. When anxiety was great within me, your consolation brought joy to my soul." Note that his consoling words replace anxiety with joy!

My favorite verse regarding Principle Number One was in Isaiah 40:29-31: "He gives strength to the weary (that was me) and increases the power of the weak (I loved that). Even youths grow tired and weary, and young men stumble and fall; but those who hope in the Lord (those who listen) will renew their strength (power)." If we listen, he gives power! It was then the Spirit said, "David, *be aggressive with this power!*" This was **Principle Number Two**.

I heard an old preacher say that all Christians spiritually posture themselves in one of four attitudes. They're either on the offense, the defense, in a state of détente (calling a truce), or running in retreat. The first one, offense, didn't apply to me very often, and for a while, the last one, retreat, seemed to be my only course of action. It's tragic that so many Christians live so much of their lives as if they were the losers rather than the winners.

That same old saint quoted Matthew 16:18 (KJV) where it says, "The gates of hell shall not prevail against you (the Church)." Then he said something to this effect: "To watch some Christians in their approach to life, you'd think the gates of hell had jumped off their hinges and were chasing them. But hell's gates don't charge God's children; God's children *charge the gates!*"

Now I heard the Holy Spirit saying, "The Father doesn't want you emotionally healed just so you can cope. He wants you healed so you can *conquer!*" The words really hit me. I needed a new mindset. I'd been on the run instead of on the charge!

The Spirit went a step further: "David, not only do we want you to be on the offense, we want you to plan ahead. And we want you to *look forward to your next opportunity.*" This was **Principle Number Three**.

"Pardon me?" I queried.

"That's right. Look forward to your next opportunity. Say 'I look forward to it.'"

Now for me, the next obvious opportunity for emotional battle was the coming Sunday morning. Oddly enough, although I had been in the ministry off and on for almost a dozen years, there were still moments when I feared public speaking. As an assistant, then associate pastor, I had often attempted to avoid speaking. I had, on occasion, told God, "I don't like this job." I had been asked to speak the next Sunday, and now, with memories of my recent panic attacks, the Holy Spirit was asking me to "look forward to it." But, I didn't look forward to it.

"Go ahead, David ... say you look forward to it."

Thoroughly puzzled, but compliant, I said the words, "I, uh, I ... I look, uhhhh, forwardtoit," making the last three words into one quick one.

The Spirit paused, wrinkled up his face somewhat and likewise ran three words into one: "Whatwasthat?"

I cleared my throat and swallowed.

"Again," he said.

"Uh, I look forward ... to ... it?"

Now leaning on one elbow, he smiled and motioned with the first two fingers on his right hand as if to draw the words out of my mouth one more time.

I picked up on his signal and cleared my throat again, "I ... look ... forward ... toit."

One more time the smile; one more time the signal. I was beginning to get his message.

"I look forward to it." It shocked me how certain I had just sounded. He smiled and signaled a third time.

"I ... *I look forward to it!*" No more signal, just a smile. "*I look forward to it!*"

After I don't know how many more jubilant I-look-forward-to-its, he stuck both hands in the air as if to imply, "You can stop now."

"I looook ..." I stopped mid-sentence.

In a matter of moments, my attitude had changed. I was surprised at how different I felt. All of a sudden, a profound confidence surged through me, and I actually *was* looking forward to it!

The Spirit smiled one last time and disappeared.

I looked back at those words in Romans 8:5-6, reading them over several more times: "Those who live in accordance with the Spirit have their minds set on what the Spirit desires.... The mind controlled by the Spirit is life and peace."

I flipped the page and skipped to verses fourteen and fifteen: "Those who are led by the Spirit of God are sons of God. For you did not receive a spirit that makes you a slave again to fear, but you received the Spirit of sonship." My eyes scanned down to verse thirty-seven: "In all these things we are more than conquerors through him who loved us."

Incredible! We, the sons and daughters, have been released from the prison of insecurity and fear. Through the Spirit of son- and daughtership, we have the authority to push back the enemy and enter a wonderful new dimension of peace, power, and emotional control!

So ended morning one.

Chapter 15

Soul Talk

My soul is full of trouble and my life draws near the grave.
— Psalm 88:3

———

*L*ater that same afternoon, I was challenged to practice the first three principles the Holy Spirit had delivered to me. As I ran down the familiar country road north of our subdivision, I could see the old foreboding cemetery almost a mile ahead of me crouching low and lying in wait. My eyes dropped to watch the gray onrushing asphalt move with indifference beneath my feet. I was confronting the fear of death once more. After nervously jogging another fifty yards, I got irritated — really irritated. *What the hell's the matter with me?* I wondered, in a not-so-Christian way. Then it hit me: Hell was *precisely* the matter here. *Come on, David,* I said to myself. *Get it together. You're the Father's son!*

With angry resolve, I lifted my head and picked up my pace. Glaring at my nearing adversary, I set my jaw and growled deep inside. With an overwhelming passion to submit my full self to the Father and to deny the enemy any further pleasure, I lifted my head toward the sky and proclaimed, "This is *your* spirit, this is *your* soul, this is *your* body ... for your kingdom, for your glory!"

With both hands on my chest, at a pounding stride, I repeated the words, this time shouting, "This is *your* spirit, this is *your* soul, this is *your* body ... for your kingdom, for your glory!" A third time, now with my clenched fists raised high, I yelled even louder — for all hell to hear, "THIS IS *HIS* SPIRIT, THIS IS *HIS* SOUL, THIS IS *HIS* BODY ... FOR HIS KINGDOM, FOR HIS GLORY!" A fourth time, a fifth — I kept chanting the phrase. I could swear I heard a fearful scream of retreat as I charged the enemy's lines.

It was amazing! It was awesome! The fear was gone! As I ran by the graveyard, my whole being tingling with power, I shouted in triumph, "I'm *your* son! I'm *your* son!"

With tears on my face, I kept running north, and I whispered the words "I'm your son."

As I lay in bed late that night, I pondered the lessons of my unusual day. The messages of the morning and the late afternoon cemetery moments were now merging together with teaching I had heard some time before, teaching on the spirit, soul, and body of man.

It is spirit, soul, and body which essentially define man as a triune being. Though most theologians agree on what a body is, there has long been varying doctrinal interpretations concerning the exact definition and function of the spirit and soul. Not being a theologian, I don't feel qualified to take an absolute position on the issue; however, the following view has worked for me.

The spirit of man is the arena of man's will, or volition, and its function is to lead the emotions. The spirit is the governmental center of man, the part of us that makes choices and decisions. The spirit could be called "the parent within us." The spirit in us has final authority over the soul *unless* it forfeits its authority by moving out from under Father God's authority and ceases to be compliant to his life principles.

The soul, on the other hand, is the center of our emotions. It's the part of us that generates feelings like love, hate, peace or fear. It could be called, as some would say, "the child within us."

Believe it or not, the soul, like a child, actually wants to be under the leadership of the "parent" spirit — if the "parent" spirit makes good decisions, that is. If the emotions seem to be out of control, "ruling the roost," so to speak, it's because our "parent" spirit hasn't been living under the authority of the Father and his principles and has, therefore, been doing a lousy job of leading our "soul child."

The activities of the soul can have direct influence and authority over the body. A simple example of this is when sudden excitement or fear triggers the release of adrenalin, in turn causing the body to respond, like the time I thought I encountered a grizzly one night while sleeping alone in the woods. It was a grouse (a mountain chicken — how fitting), but my soul kept my body awake all night. My spirit was the only thing that slept.

An interesting note: A book entitled *None of These Diseases* by Doctors S. I. McMillen and David Stern states that about eighty percent of all sicknesses can be tied to emotional stimuli (which is why if you have high blood pressure the doctor may ask if you are under a lot of stress). The soul is a powerful part of us for better or for worse depending on the condition of our spirit.

The body, the visible member of the trio, is merely the frame-work for, and is subject to, the soul or the spirit, depending upon who's taking charge at the moment.

Now, back to the spirit and soul. It's amazing how many people, including many Christians, don't understand the dual dynamic that exists inside. Whatever you call these two parts in us, they each play a very distinctive role. You are not *one* confused and conflicted person. In effect, there are two of you in that body. It's natural to hear the strong voice of the soul inside. Now it's time our spirit learns to do some talking back! We need to do a little "soul talk." For example: "Come on, David, remember — you're the Father's son!"

The Psalmist did this on several occasions. One verse that comes to mind became a popular worship chorus: "Praise the Lord, O my soul; all my inmost being, praise his holy name" (Psalm 103:1). King David knew there was an emotional "other" within him that needed to be motivated once in a while. Soul talk.

Another example of David's soul talk is Psalm 43:5: "Why are you downcast, O my soul? Why so disturbed within me? Put your hope in God, for I will yet praise him." Here's a man's spirit, submitted to God's Spirit, giving some pretty sound leadership to an emotionally-upset soul. And my bet is that his body's blood pressure went back down. Soul talk!

The first step, before the soul talk, is to make sure you've submitted your spirit to God's, "having your *mind set* on what the Spirit desires." This is dependency in action, and it reconnects your whole triune being into the Creator's unique and wonderful chain of command. Your spirit responding to the counsel of God's Spirit is the key to restoring creation order to your spirit, soul, and body.

I believe understanding the relationship between the special functions of the spirit, soul, and body can be tremendously beneficial in dealing with emotions, which, in turn, can positively affect your process of maturity.

———

In the fall of 1989, we witnessed our daughter, Kimberly, putting this understanding to work. It was in Butte, Montana, one year after Kimberly won the title of Montana Junior Miss. She had been flown back to Montana from Troy, Alabama, where she was attending university on a Junior Miss scholarship, to serve as guest of honor at the 1989 Montana Junior Miss competition.

It was one of Kimberly's jobs to coach and encourage the girls as they prepared for the big event at the end of the week. Kimberly would also take an active role in the program singing two special songs, giving a final farewell speech, and presenting the traditional bouquet of roses to the lucky winner late Saturday night.

Kathy and I were excited to get a few days away and see Kimi. It had been some months since we had last been together. We were missing her, and she was fighting a lot of homesickness. Now, we would get to see her during some of the practice sessions and a few other times here and there over the long weekend.

Late Saturday morning is when our little episode began. Kathy and I were in the large Butte auditorium as observers for the final dress rehearsal. Kathy was visiting with someone on our left, and I was watching what was happening on stage. While a host of teenage girls were in a frenzy over their assignments, I couldn't help but notice Kimi engaged in what appeared to be a fairly serious conversation with the program director and orchestra leader.

After a few minutes, Kimi turned and looked our way. When her eyes caught mine, she made a beeline for the steps at my far right, made a quick descent, crossed in front of the stage, and headed straight for me. When she reached me and we stood face to face, I could see her eyes were a little watery.

"Daddy," she said, with a little tremble in her voice, "I need to get your counsel."

"Sure, honey, what is it?"

"Daddy, do you remember me telling you and Mom about Wendy, the 1986 Montana Junior Miss who died of cancer three months ago?"

"Yes, Kimi, it was a very sad story."

"Well, tonight they're going to do a special memorial presentation in her honor. At a certain point in the evening, her family will be escorted down to the front row to sit next to you and Mom. Wendy's mom and dad, her grandparents, and several other family members will be here. After the two emcees give a tribute to her life, they want all the girls, dressed in their formals, on the stage in a big semi-circle. The orchestra will start to play, and then they want me to come downstage, take the microphone, and sing the song 'Friends Are Friends Forever' in dedication to Wendy. Dad, I don't think I can make it through the song."

Then I understood the tears. It was a sad song to listen to let alone sing in front of a grieving family and a thousand unsuspecting sympathizers.

I looked deep into my little girl's eyes and held both of her hands. I paused briefly and said, "Kimi, this is a very powerful song, and all of those who will be here tonight need to *hear* the words. God wants every one of them to hear the words. Now, here's what to do. Sing the song *seriously*; don't sing it *emotionally*. Okay?" I was trying to give Kimi quick, practical counsel on spirit-over-soul management.

She looked at me, broke into a smile, hugged me hard around the neck and said, "Thank you, Daddy," and trotted back up on stage.

I turned away, misty-eyed and heavy-hearted, fighting to hold back *my* emotions. My soul couldn't take it.

The evening came and everyone was dressed in their finest. At the designated moment, Wendy's whole family was escorted down the aisle. Kathy greeted and hugged a tearful mother; I shook hands with a tearful dad. We all were seated and the memorial began.

One of the emcees was a local businesswoman, refined and sincere. She was a former Winter Olympic athlete and an outspoken Christian. She held herself together extremely well during the memorial. Her counterpart, a local deejay, didn't fare so well. Several times during the presentation, he seemed quite choked up. It was hard not to get choked up, however. This Wendy had been a special young woman, and she was taken away at such a young age.

Finally the orchestra began to play; all the girls held hands in the semicircle and Kimi stepped forward. Kathy and I held hands too, but for different reasons. I also held my breath as Kimberly began to sing.

I could hardly believe what I heard. Since the time Kimi was a little girl she loved to sing. I had heard her sing countless times, but never in my life had I heard her sing like this. She was powerful. She was absolutely anointed with such clarity and tone her song seemed to suddenly push me back in my seat. I was blown away.

I noticed right away the man on my right began pulling a handkerchief out of his sport-coat pocket. The woman to his right began pulling Kleenex out of her patent-leather purse. The man on her right took a Kleenex out of his coat. Kathy was prepared in advance; she had a pile of Kleenex already on her lap. I didn't need a Kleenex. I had a perfectly good sleeve on my sport coat. With a quick glance back, I could see flashes of Kleenex everywhere throughout the darkened auditorium.

The male emcee was wiping back tears. The girls, who were supposed to hold hands and back Kimi up on the chorus, were dropping their hands, wiping their eyes, swaying out of time; into each other instead of with each other. And this dad and so-called counselor was crying like a sprinkler.

When she finished the song, the entire audience stood to their feet and applauded for more than a minute. When the clapping stopped, someone in the back of the auditorium shouted, "Sing it again!" — and they made her sing the whole song again! And once more: Kleenex everywhere.

By the time it was over, it was apparent that it was the audience that had not been able to "make it through the song."

There was only one young woman that night without a tear in her eyes — the one who sang from down in her spirit, not from her soul.

Dear brothers and sisters, connect with your heavenly Counselor. Sing your life song from your spirit, and hear your soul applaud!

Chapter 16

An Electric Rainbow

*In your hands are strength and power to exalt and give
strength to all.*
— 1 Chronicles 29:12

———

*A*s I sat down at my desk early on the second morning of our
unique encounters, the Visitor in the orange Naugahyde chair
turned his head slowly to his left and looked in the direction of
my closed office door. There, in front of the door, I could see another
one of those "visions."

Now at this point, if you want to bail out of this book, I
wouldn't blame you too much. However, you're into it this far, so why
not keep going?

Ah, you're staying with me! I appreciate it.

Right there, just inside my office door, I saw, in my mind's eye,
the presence of Jesus. Hold on now! He was standing there with his
arms stretched toward me, and from out of his hands came an *electric
rainbow* — a rainbow of colorful light and power that arced over the

top of my desk. With the crackling sound of lightning, it bolted into and exploded throughout my whole being! I jolted upright in my chair with a feeling of emotional strength I had never known before.

"Holy mackerel!" I blurted out in complete astonishment as I turned toward the Spirit. He was smiling. "David," he said, *"practice his presence."* This was **Principle Number Four**.

The Scripture that came to me was Psalm 25:15: "My eyes are ever on the Lord, for only he will release my feet from the snare." He wants us to see his presence, and when we do, he will rescue us from our emotional trauma!

Another verse is in Psalm 59:9: "O my Strength, I *watch* for you; you, O God, are my fortress." When we see him, we will receive his strength!

Almost every Christian knows and can quote the Scripture where Jesus said, "And surely *I am with you always*, to the very end of the age" (Matthew 28:20). Yet how many actually believe in and acknowledge his real presence? He's really there with you with real strength to replace your emotional weakness! This is true even when people are threatening you. Look at this verse, Psalm 109:31: "For *he stands at the right hand of the needy one*, to save his life from those who condemn him." Remember: When you're feeling needy or afraid, when you're challenged by memories or your present circumstances, *practice his presence*. It works!

Sunday morning came, and I was "looking forward to the opportunity" — to speak in church, that is. Yep, I woke up and right away told my soul I was looking forward to the opportunity. It (my soul) started to make a case for terror, but I just kept on saying, "I look forward to the opportunity." All the way to church, while engaged in car-ride type conversation, I secretly mumbled orders under my breath: "I'm looking forward to the opportunity." My soul was now trying the simple anxiety angle, so I soul-talked all the way into the church parking lot.

By the time I walked through the church doors, my "soul partner" inside was actually calm, looking forward to the opportunity.

But just to make sure, I repeated the phrase several more times until the moment arrived for me to take the pulpit.

It was great! I had never remembered feeling so relaxed and at ease when speaking. Everything was going fine until about half way through my message when "we" suddenly *stopped* looking forward to it! I don't know how it happened, but right there, in the middle of my sermon, I lost it, and my soul partner started freaking out. It was back to terror.

As I stood there, knees knocking, before the entire congregation, I drew a complete blank and went thoroughly speechless. Sweat began forming on my forehead as I fought to remember what in the world I was talking about. Now, fear can cause one's imagination to get super creative, so it appeared to me all my dear friends were growing horns on top of their heads. I imagined that at any minute they would begin throwing hymnals or something at me.

I thought for a moment about pulling the list of Spirit-given principles out of my wallet and reading over them for help, but then I thought it might seem strange to take a five-minute reading break right in the middle of my message. I also thought about taking some Valium, but I knew the drug would take at least a half hour to work, and by that time everyone would have thrown the hymnals for sure.

Suddenly, I remembered! I scanned the auditorium — and there he was. Way in the very back of the sanctuary, right behind sweet old Esther Hogue in the last row, I saw Jesus standing. Out of his hands came the rainbow of light and power arcing with magnificent colored energy above Esther's head, charging right at and into me. (You think I'm kidding, don't you?) In an instant, I snapped to attention. I became absolutely fearless and jumped back on board my train of thought. It was great! His presence gave me immediate, commanding confidence, just as it had in the office.

So many times since that Sunday morning, I have practiced this principle; I have practiced his presence. Once, while I was on a flight across the Pacific Ocean, the plane started rocking hard at thirty-five thousand feet, and I started tensing up. I remembered the Spirit's words once again: "David, *practice his presence.*" I looked up and saw Jesus standing there next to the in-flight movie screen with his hands outstretched and that rainbow flowing out of his hands and flooding into me. I completely relaxed; the fear was gone. Time after time, he has been there, and every time I see him the fear is gone.

Now, for the sake of clarification, I'm certainly not saying you need to see a rainbow to be spiritual or have emotional control. Though God did make rainbows and they are biblically sound, seeing one is not a criterion for mental health. On the contrary, "seeing things," as you've no doubt heard, generally doesn't produce a very positive mental diagnosis. But, irrespective of the differing opinions of the mental health community, I believe there is one thing that's very healthy to see: the caring, strengthening presence of the Father, Son, and Holy Spirit.

Remember, this isn't about religion — it's about relationship; mutual relationship. Don't miss out! Participate in this real relationship by *hearing* him and *seeing* him. Choose with your spirit to hear and see, and you'll begin to experience new peace and power!

Chapter 17

A Loving Order

*But now, this is what the Lord says ... "Fear not, for I have
redeemed you; I have summoned you by name."*
— Isaiah 43:1

———

*T*he Spirit paused briefly during the encounter in my office,
making sure he had my attention, and proceeded to give me
Principle Number Five. He said these words: "David, *do not
be anxious.*" He paused once more, smiled with compassion, and added,
"And that's an order."

"Pardon me?" I flinched at his words.

The Spirit continued smiling kindly, waiting for me to get the
message.

Then it hit me. The Bible speaks on the issue of fear and
anxiety numerous times, and never once does God simply *ask* us not to
fear or *suggest* we try not to be anxious. He says, in effect, *don't do it!*
His words on the issue always come in the form of an imperative statement, a directive; in other words, a command. God would never

command us to do something we didn't have the ability to do. Think about that. Anxiety is another emotion within our control. We can make a choice by our spirit — our will — to obey his command and be rid of fear.

I not only got the message, I loved it. I had lived for so long at the whim of anxiety; thinking if it was there, it was there, and there wasn't much I could do about it. All of a sudden, dealing with anxiety became a matter of *obedience*. The Father doesn't want us to be anxious. I had never thought of it before, but anxiety doesn't please him. Why? First of all, because he loves us, and he's always concerned for our well-being. Our choice to remain anxious cripples our well-being, keeping us in a state of spiritual, emotional, and physical jeopardy. Second, we are actually telling him with our anxiety that we don't fully trust him.

The solution? We ask for forgiveness for not trusting him, and then we obey him. He tells us not to fear and we respond. We say, "Yes, Father." It's simple and it works. Once again, if we put our trust in our Father and take action with our spirit, then he will begin to fill us with new emotions of confidence and peace.

My eyes fell on the Scripture Isaiah 41:10: "*Do not fear*, for I am with you; *do not be dismayed* (anxious), for I am your God. I will strengthen you and help you." I read those words over several times. They gave me chills and brought tears to my eyes at the same time. The ancient words were making me feel stronger than I had ever felt before.

I thought to look next at the Old Testament book of Joshua. I hadn't realized it before, but it seems Joshua, the great commander of the Israelite army, apparently also suffered with issues of fear. From reading chapter one, I suspect he allowed his anxiety to show on more than one occasion. Several times in that chapter, he is ordered by God and then reminded again, to be "strong and courageous." Joshua 1:6 says: "Be strong and courageous, because you will lead these people to inherit the land." Verse seven: "Be strong and very courageous." Verse nine: "Have I not commanded you? Be strong and courageous. Do not be terrified; do not be discouraged, for the Lord your God will be with you wherever you go." And the last words of the chapter in verse eighteen? "Only be strong and courageous!"

So, what was God's message to Joshua and to each of us? Be strong and courageous! If we obey him, and if we choose strength and courage, he will empower us. It's our choice.

There's no better story than the story of Joshua to demonstrate Principle Number Five: *Do not be anxious*. Joshua listened, Joshua obeyed; with a spirit of courage, Joshua conquered. Many interpret courage to be a feeling. Courage may, in time, be accompanied with feelings of confidence, but courage itself is not a feeling, it's a choice. Joshua chose not to be anxious. He chose to be courageous.

Now, I would never dare say I have always made the right choice. I'm still challenged at times by fear. Sometimes I let it get to me for a short while, but then he reminds me: "Don't be afraid, son … don't be afraid."

Yes, Father.

Chapter 18

Never Fear Man

*The Lord is with me; I will not be afraid. What can man do
to me?*
— Psalm 118:6

———

Next came **Principle Number Six**: *Never fear man.*

I heard a story about a pastor who walked out of a church building late one Sunday morning after most of his congregation had gone home, and headed for his car in the nearly-empty church parking lot. As he approached his car, he noticed an unfamiliar vehicle parked next to it. When he got to his car and inserted the key into the door, a man, who had been hiding in the unfamiliar vehicle, suddenly jumped out, pulled a gun, pointed it at the pastor's face and said, "Pastor, today you're gonna die."

The pastor looked the gunman in the eye and said, "Mister, if today is my day to die, then by all means pull the trigger. But if it isn't, then I must warn you — you are in very great danger."

I never heard what happened to the gunman, but the pastor lived to tell the story. The pastor was right, you know. It was the gunman who was "in danger." He was the one who was not under the care of the heavenly Father.

When the Spirit shared the "never fear man" principle, he said, "David, you are a son of the Father. Understanding the significance and authority of this position results in fearlessness. Why should you — a fearless son — fear those who are not sons and fearful?"

I didn't know. Why?

I thought about it some more. He was *right!* There are none who can stand with more assurance than the sons and daughters of God!

I thought again of that old familiar Scripture in the sonship chapter, Romans 8:28: "And we know that in all things God works for the good of those who love him." No matter what happens in life, including those things we don't like or understand, the Father always champions his children. Regardless of the tough challenges along the way, the children will ultimately experience that all things *do* work together for their good.

The same chapter goes on to say in verse 31: "If God is for us, who can be against us?" And I love the words in verses 35-39:

> Who shall separate us from the love of Christ? Shall trouble or hardship or persecution or famine or nakedness or danger or sword?… No, in all these things we are more than conquerors through him who loved us. For I am convinced that neither death nor life, neither angels nor demons, neither present nor the future, nor any powers, neither height nor depth, nor anything else in all creation, will be able to separate us from the love of God that is in Christ Jesus our Lord.

Shortly after I became a youth pastor for a large church in Southern California, Kathy and I had the privilege of hearing Corrie Ten Boom speak in our church just a few years before her death. By then, the former prisoner of war, Holocaust survivor, and author of *The Hiding Place* was a very feeble, shaky old woman, standing simple and bow-legged before thousands in our Sunday evening service.

I could see from my seat near the front of the large auditorium that there was a house fly (I suppose it was a church fly) buzzing around her head the entire time she was speaking. She kept lifting her feeble arm and waving away at the thing with her bony fingers every time it landed on her forehead or nose.

I was getting really bugged. *Dang fly*, I thought. *Poor, poor Corrie. She's so ...* Before I could get the next thought out of my sympathetic soul, a voice somewhere inside interrupted: *"Don't say 'poor Corrie.' When my daughter, Corrie, walks through international airports, the demons run away from her, shrieking in terror!"*

No matter what their size, shape, gender, color, intelligence, health, or age; there are none who are more loved and have more authority than we children of the King. And there is nothing and no one who can separate us from the Father's loving caregiving and power.

There are far too many Christians who allow themselves to be dominated physically and/or emotionally by one or more individuals because of the fear of man and a wrong assessment of their own significance. The longer one thinks of himself or herself as a doormat, the longer he or she will continue to get stepped on. It's sad to say there are also too many wonderful Christian women who, burdened with low self-assessments and doctrinally-faulty, pressure-filled teaching, are extremely unhappy and don't understand why. And there is at least an equal amount of insecure and misdirected men who take advantage of these women.

I don't want to focus on just the women here. There are really as many male victims as there are female. The fear of man has no gender preference. Moreover, whether couched in domination or subordination, the fear of man eventually makes everyone a victim. Fear of any kind is innately controlling and, in time, self-destructive.

While there are appropriate times for submission here on earth, any submission to people must be approved and empowered by our Father, with whom we have a *straight-line relationship*. Therefore, we never submit to anyone out of fear and weakness. We only submit out of the authority, power, and complete security that is ours as the Father's sons or daughters.

Consider this, married couples: As we have already said, if you are Christians, you are a son and daughter of the Father, a son and daughter of the King. Both of you are of great stature and worthy of equal honor. Let your imagination run a little wild for a minute, and imagine the two of you as a prince and princess riding happily together atop the King's carriage, which is accompanied by angelic soldiers and moving down a beautiful country road. It is a gorgeous day in the King's kingdom.

One of you sits on one side of the King, one on the other side. Both of you are nobility, so you carry yourselves with the dignity befitting your honored positions. Both of you are submitted to this loving King above all else, and both of you fear no one. You live under the King's protective caregiving. Though the two of you have different giftings and roles in the King's kingdom, you each have the most wonderful sense of significance, well-being, and purpose.

The first key to a successful marriage is for each partner to give their spouse equal honor. Husband, you should see yourself as a son of the King, being first submitted to him. Then, honor your wife for the daughter of the King she is. Wife, you should see yourself as daughter of the King, being first submitted to him. Then honor your husband for the son of the King he is.

What if your partner isn't a Christian? Show your partner the same kind of love and honor the loving King would. What if your partner, Christian or not, wants you to do something against the King's principles? You still show honor and respect to your partner, but you do what the King wants you to do. What if your partner dishonors and mistreats you? Look at the King, your loving and protective Father who sits between you, receive the honor *he* gives you, and ask him what you should do next. You might be surprised at what he will say.

You must always submit securely out of your position of power as the Father's daughter or son, never out of weakness, never out of fear. If your submission comes out of weakness or fear, it's not godly submission. You have made yourself a doormat. Controllers, by the way, whether they are men or women, never respect doormats. They disdain them. However, a controller needs someone to control, someone to serve his or her own selfish purposes. The Father doesn't want any of his children to be controlled. To be controlled is to be abused.

The world's answer to the abused is often to encourage them to seek and demonstrate power of their own, but this reactionary tactic only demonstrates a *false* power and is a thin disguise for the root problem: the fear of man. False power — which is actually nurtured by the fear of man and usually accompanied with anger, revenge, and/or intellectual enlightenment and detachment — will also prove self-destructive.

Many think they no longer have the fear of man simply because they have taken a reactive position against and/or have perhaps avoided certain individuals. In truth, unless we learn to take a pro-active position of peace and strength in sonship or daughtership, we remain victimized by the fear of man and spiritually vulnerable. Proverbs 29:25 says, "Fear of man will prove to be a snare (a trap), but whoever trusts in the Lord is kept safe." We need to remember that bringing reactive judgment against anyone else will more than likely backfire on us. Most are familiar with the verse in Matthew 7:1: "Do not judge, or you too will be judged."

However you look at it, whether functioning emotionally or physically on the offense or defense, we are under a powerful, controlling force when affected by the fear of man.

The Father didn't create us to be *under* control. He created us in his likeness, to live with him in his peaceful and loving realm of caregiving. He created us to make personal, free, and creative choices without being dominated by someone else. It was, as I said earlier, his original and then redemptive intention that we thoroughly experience the freedom and security of our unique significance as his children.

Step out of the controlling bondage of the fear of man and embrace the tremendous, God-given authority, peace, power, and happiness meant for you as a son or daughter of the heavenly Father.

Chapter 19

Relax ... And Live Your Life!

Be at rest once more, O my soul, for the Lord has been good to you.
— Psalm 116:7

———

nd then came **Principle Number Seven.** "David," the Spirit said, "*relax*. Be deliberate instead of reactive. Pause ... slow down ... take control ... *live*."

The words hit home. For too long, my modus operandi had been one of crisis management — knee-jerky. It wasn't uncommon for me to knock over a glass of water at a local restaurant and then, in a quick attempt to clean it up, dump my soup. On the way out, for extra measure, I might collide with a senior citizen who was on portable oxygen. Generally speaking, I was an accident waiting to happen.

It was also not uncommon for me to feel I had to provide an answer for every question, even if the question was directed at someone else. I had always felt obliged to keep the conversation going, be everybody's friend, and laugh convincingly at jokes I didn't like or get. I would sometimes apologize for things I didn't do or that never even happened. I often felt guilty for having fun. And then, of course, it wasn't fun, because I felt guilty for it.

The next words out of the Spirit's mouth had a profound impact on me, and I will remember them all the days of my life. "David," he said, "you take yourself *way* too seriously."

Ouch! I gulped. I knew what he meant. I had been a person of continual self-evaluation and unhealthy introspection. I just never felt good enough. I could never come to a place of rest with myself. I was constantly searching for significance, all the while enforcing an unattractive self-pride.

I was in shock for several moments, impacted by the words. Then my eyes filled with tears as I pondered the truth. At first, the tears came over regret for the past. Then tears came over hope for the future. Right there, in my office, I began to feel a huge burden lift off my emotional shoulders. I began to understand. It was time for me to *relax* — and it was time for me to *live* my life.

Many Christians are under the same sort of burden I was. Perhaps they express it differently than I did, but their bottom line is the same — no life. Some, for example, feel if they aren't doing something for God every minute then they aren't pleasing him. They operate as though there is no time and seldom any grace for oneself.

I have known Christian workers who, when they hear of a need somewhere else in the world, feel a great sense of responsibility to go there and meet the need, even though they are already serving in an important ministry capacity. They feel torn in different directions, as if they should be omnipresent. An experienced saint once said, "The need does not necessitate the call." Yet many Christian workers are troubled by every need they become aware of when the need is not theirs to meet.

Some feel they have suddenly impaired their relationship with God if they miss a prayer or quiet time. Remember, quiet times weren't intended for the purpose of building God up, but for the purpose of building us up. To keep on growing, we'll need time with the Father for the rest of our lives, but he doesn't get angry with us if we sometimes break our devotional routine. We need to see God for who he really is. This relationship is about a Father and his children, not a warden and his prisoners.

The Father is not needy, demanding, or self-centered. He lacks in nothing; his nature is love, and being the ultimate Being, without any need for a caregiver of his own, his only concern is for others. He actually lives who he is and what he preaches. For example, take the passages "God is love" and "It is more blessed to give than to receive." Though having loving children does bring the Father great pleasure, most of his pleasure comes from his giving *them* pleasure and seeing *them* happy. All good and loving parents feel this way, and God is the author of good and loving parenting.

Follow with me as I illustrate, in human terms, his fatherly nature when it concerns our happiness. Suppose you have a daughter, and you take her to McDonalds for a special treat. When you get in line to order, you ask your daughter, "What would you like to eat, sweetheart?" And suppose she responds, "What would you like me to have, Daddy?" And you say, "Sweetheart, I would like you to have whatever you want to have." Then she says, "But Daddy, I only want what you want me to have, and you probably want me to have a fish sandwich because you know I don't like fish sandwiches, and I want you to be happy with me, so I will have a fish sandwich ... and can I please have some water?"

Contrary to some doctrines, God is not a "fish sandwich" God. At the risk of sounding repetitive, he really does love to see us happy. He *longs* for the day when there is no more sorrow and all of his children experience nothing but perpetual happiness. He works *for* our happiness, not against it! Therefore (please listen, dear Christian workers), being the Father he is, it's in his nature to say, "Give my little girl anything on the menu she wants — *plus* a chocolate shake!"

After a few minutes, the Spirit leaned forward, smiled, and said, "Son, put down that Bible and let's go fishing."

Wow! He wanted me *to live life!*

Years later, I was driving home from a teaching trip in Southern Alberta, Canada. It was my last trip of the year, and I was so happy to be going home for the Christmas holidays. As much as I like doing what I do, most of all I love coming home to Kathy, the kids, and now the grand kids. Living in the mountains of Montana is the icing on the cake.

After crossing the U.S./Canadian border, my route had taken me west on the Highline, through the Blackfeet Indian Reservation, and into the little town of Browning at the base of the Rockies on the east side of the Continental Divide. I continued west on Highway 2 and sped up the eastern slopes heading toward East Glacier, the eastern entrance to Glacier National Park. About three miles from the summit of Marias Pass, I was suddenly engulfed in a most unusual and spectacular winter display. A snowfall the night before had left ten inches of fresh new powder. Though the road had been plowed, it was packed hard and white, nearly blending with the adjacent and luminous snowfields that pushed back the dense forest a few hundred yards off the highway's edges.

The sun was brilliant, and the gigantic, snow-covered peaks ahead of me glistened against a gorgeous blue Montana "big sky." But what stole the show was the fresh, finely-powdered snow being carried by the high winds. With powerful, symphonic movements, the powder danced magically back and forth across the snow packed surface of the highway.

Now, the entire roadway before me had become one with the snowfields — a flurry of swirling white. I felt exactly like I was flying on a cloud. It was incredible! I powered down all four windows on my old Honda Accord and turned up my Kenny G tape to nearly full volume. I thought I heard the Father say, *"Go faster!"*

Not wanting to disobey, I dropped from fifth gear into fourth and charged through the pass and over the top of the world! The mountains, the motion, the music, the moment … all so wonderful, so free. Close to the summit, I finally let go a shout at the top of my lungs: "Father! This is *beautiful!*"

I distinctly heard him reply, "I thought you'd like this."

That was my only conversation with God that day, and it was sweet.

We love him. We serve him. He loves us. He wants us to live our lives!

Chapter 20

Praise

*I will extol the Lord at all times; his praise will always be on
my lips.*
— Psalm 34:1

———

*P*rinciple **Number Eight**: *Choose to praise,* and step out of your
introspection.

I started playing the guitar when I was about eleven
years old. In my ruckus years, it was my sidekick at beach parties. Later,
after committing my life as a Christian, it became an instrument for
praise and worship gatherings. It's strange how things go sometimes,
isn't it?

I have always enjoyed playing or just singing along in praise and
worship with any size group. For several years, I led worship in the
church where I was an associate pastor.

At one point in my worship-leading days, I had to stop and ask
the question (by the way, God is not at all offended by honest questions and, in fact, encourages them), "Father, why do you ask your

children to worship you? I know you're not selfish, proud, or self-centered. I know these things are not part of your character. So why *do* you ask for worship? I wouldn't ask my children to worship me."

This is what I heard him say:

"Ah, but David, think about that for a minute. How many times have you asked your children if they loved you, or how about the times when you encouraged them to tell their mommy they loved her? How many times have you asked your children to give you a hug? How many times have you asked them to sit on your lap?"

I was beginning to understand.

"And who benefits most from the sitting-on-the-lap experience?" he continued.

"Mmmm, now I see. *They* do. But, *I* love it, too."

"So do I, son … so do I."

Praise and worship is all about a loving relationship — a relationship in which both the Father and his children benefit, but one in which the children benefit the most. Praise and worship is actually one of the Father's ways of connecting with us in emotional love. It's another context in which he encourages us. On his lap, in the place of praise and worship, we forget about our doubts and fears; we come out of our introspection and enter into a restoring mutuality. It's on his lap the Father reminds us of our significance and gives us new strength. Praise and worship are gifts of love from the Father to his children, and he loves it when we use them.

I love Psalm 40:2-3: "He lifted me out of the slimy pit, out of the mud and mire; he set my feet on a rock and gave me a firm place to stand. He put a new song in my mouth, a hymn of praise to our God. Many will see and fear and put their trust in the Lord."

He rescues us, gives us a brand new song to sing, and then, note the last line: "Many (others) will see and put their trust in the Lord." As I thought on those words, I realized that expressing love to the Father through praise, especially in the difficult times, also benefits third parties in this relationship: our brothers and sisters who still lie in the desert places, desperate for a reason to sing. Our praise and worship inspires them to move toward his lap where they, too, can discover their significance and be empowered.

In this final passage, note the *soul talk* and the choice to praise God: "Why are you in despair, O my soul? Why are you so disturbed within me? Hope in God, for I shall again praise him!" (Psalm 43:5 NASB).

"David, don't despair anymore … *choose to praise.*"

"Yes, Lord … yes."

Chapter 21

Warfare

*Finally, be strong in the Lord and in his mighty power. Put on
the full armor of God so that you can take your stand
against the devil's schemes. For our struggle is not against
flesh and blood, but against the rulers, against the authorities,
against the powers of this dark world and against the spiritual
forces of evil in the heavenly realms.*
— Ephesians 6:10-12

*P*rinciple **Number Nine**: "David, *spiritual warfare ... be the
warrior.*"
The Spirit didn't say a lot about this topic, so neither
will I. He simply reminded me once again that we have a very real
enemy out there, and we need to stay strong. The Bible calls that
enemy the devil, and he is committed to one thing: His full time
mission is to prevent as many human beings as possible from becoming
the Father's children. He's furious that he lost his significance when he
was removed from God's kingdom, and he doesn't want us to have any

significance either. And so our enemy *schemes*. He makes up secret and devious plans to divert us.

Paul tells us in Ephesians that we can do something about the devil's devices. First, we need to be aware that scheming is going on. It's easy to forget this. I know from personal experience that sometimes we don't even *consider* the possibility that some troubles could be the result of the enemy's schemes. In short, we should remember that he plots against us, and then, stay on guard.

Second, we need to recognize the authority we have to take a "stand against the devil's schemes." Jesus, the first born Son, was given this authority, and so were his brothers and sisters — you and I. For the rest of our lives, we must remember who we are and "be strong in the Lord and his mighty power!"

Another Scripture that came to me was James 4:7: "Submit yourselves, then, to God. Resist the devil, and he will flee from you." That's exactly what I did when I ran, *shouting to the heavenly realms*, past the old graveyard — I submitted to God and resisted the enemy. And that's what I've done many times since.

Being a warrior is as simple as this: Stay in mutuality with the Father and tell the enemy to back off. He has no right to keep hassling a son or daughter of the King, so don't let him. Did you catch the last line of that verse in James? "He will flee from you." He will *run* from you! You have that much authority! It's part of your inheritance.

For some outstanding help on the subject of spiritual warfare, I recommend *Spiritual Warfare for Every Christian* by Dean Sherman, a respected teacher, author, and friend of mine. Dean covers the subject from stem to stern.

———

Be strong, dear friend, and *be the warrior*.

Wallet Wisdom

Wallet Wisdom From the Fascinating Person in the Orange Naugahyde Chair

Principle #1: Listen to the Father and you'll receive his power.

Principle #2: Be aggressive with this power.

Principle #3: Look forward to your next opportunity.

Principle #4: Practice his presence.

Principle #5: Do not be anxious or afraid.

Principle #6: Never fear man.

Principle #7: Relax, slow down, take control, and live.

Principle #8: Choose to praise, and step out of your introspection.

Principle #9: Put on your armor, take up your sword, and be the warrior.

Principle #10: Give your life away (just ahead: living with new purpose).

You might want to write these principles down — and put them in your wallet.

PART SIX

A New Purpose

We serve God, our Father, by embracing
his shared understanding of and
commitment to the great value of others;
those close to us and those who are not.

Chapter 22

Give Your Life Away

Give, and it will be given to you.
— Luke 6:38

⁓

*T*here was one more principle, **Principle Number Ten**, that came from the Counselor in the orange Naugahyde chair:

"David," the Spirit said, "after you have rested, *give your life away.*"

I have a personal word of encouragement for those of you who have gone through what seemed to be needless suffering. The Father loves you and is proud of you. You made it through. While you suffered, he wept for you; and while he wept, he never stopped in his efforts to vindicate you and redeem something wonderful from the debris of your trials.

You are, perhaps, like Joseph, who was sold out by family members, abused by the selfish, and left alone with no sense of hope. Like Joseph, you may have felt the depths of despair. But know this: All the while Joseph was in the pit, fearing for his life, the Father was rubbing his shoulders and whispering the words, "Hold on, boy ... hold on." And at the same time, the Father's eyes were on the nations of the earth and all the other children who would one day be affected by the life and experiences of this one son. One day, all that had once looked like ruin came rushing into meaning when Joseph was able to utter these words to the brothers who had so shamefully abused him: "You intended to harm me, but God intended it for good to accomplish what is now being done, the saving of many lives" (Genesis 50:20). Joseph was so touched by the loving and redemptive hand of the Father that he was able to go on to say, "'So then, don't be afraid. I will provide for you and your children.' And he reassured them and spoke kindly to them" (v. 21).

I can say to you, the Father will redeem the past. Even the waste will not go to waste. He remembers the pit and will be faithful to bring the reward.

In the aftermath of my own personal bit of suffering, I looked back with hard questions. Why the pain? Why did it happen? Where was the good in any of it? In a timely way, a dear friend came by one day and shared some truth that was soothing to my soul, and I will keep it with me forever. Perhaps it will be helpful to you if you have questions about the pain of the past.

My friend told me to read Psalm 84:5-7. It goes like this:

Blessed are those whose strength is in you, who have set their hearts on pilgrimage. As they pass through the Valley of Baca (weeping), they make it a place of springs (they dig wells, representing comfort); the autumn rains also cover it with pools. They go from strength to strength, till each appears before God in Zion.

"David," my friend said, "you have gone through the Valley of Baca, the place of sorrow. In your thirst for peace, you dug for answers in a desert place. You found what you longed for; you have become stronger, you have become a resource of peace and understanding, and the Father has poured out still greater blessings upon you. Because of your digging, you are now able to offer water of compassion and wisdom to many pilgrims who are still in the heat of their pilgrimage."

Somewhere I heard the saying: Knowledge comes through study, but wisdom comes through pain. So it is, my friend, your sorrow will not be wasted. Your experience can become a rich supply of hope to those coming behind you. Let your love and wisdom be water to those who still yearn for comfort. Don't hate your memories — profit from them. You are Joseph. Save some lives.

As you give your life to others, all the more life will come back to you. The Spirit led me to some Scriptures regarding this. The first one was 2 Corinthians 9:6: "Whoever sows sparingly will also reap sparingly, and whoever sews generously will also reap generously." The blessing you plant in others will even be harvested in you.

Jesus was the perfect example. Look at some highlights again in Philippians 2:5-9: "Your attitude should be the same as that of Christ Jesus: Who... taking the very nature of a servant ... humbled himself ... obedient to death ... *Therefore, God exalted him to the highest place.*" His lifestyle and final reward served as a testimony to his words in Matthew 23:12: "Whoever humbles himself will be exalted."

Whether it was fear, as in my case, or something else that that caused you pain, giving yourself away is part of the answer to over-coming that pain. I like what John said in his first letter, chapter 4:18 (actually, the body of the chapter is all about loving others as a demon-stration of our love toward God): "There is no fear in love. But perfect love drives out fear." Loving others, serving their highest good, actu-ally drives fear out of the picture — your picture and theirs.

Giving to others is not only beneficial to them, but as with praise and worship to God, it's a tremendous means by which we personally can experience healing and renewal. As Jesus said, "Give and it shall be given unto you." It's really true! There is a new dynamic of empowerment — fuel, if you will — returned to the one who serves as a supply of power to someone else. So, don't linger in your pain, sorrow, or insecurities. If you want inner healing, serve others. Begin with those closest to you, then reach beyond.

The last Scripture the Spirit gave me during those three days in my office is among my all-time favorites. Isaiah 58:10-11:

> If you spend yourselves in behalf of the hungry and satisfy the needs of the oppressed, then your light will rise in the darkness, and your night will become like the noonday. The Lord will

guide you always; he will satisfy your needs in a sun-scorched land and will strengthen your frame. *You will be like a well-watered garden, like a spring whose waters never fail.*

There's a cup of water in your hand. Give someone a drink.

Chapter 23

The Great Value of Others

For God so loved the world …
— John 3:16

———

It was six o'clock on a cold winter morning at Logan Airport in Boston, Massachusetts. I had just finished conducting a seminar the night before at a church in Manchester, New Hampshire, and I was heading home to Montana. I had managed to get only three hours of sleep and was eagerly looking forward to boarding my jet and sprawling out for a well-deserved little nap.

Much to my dismay, there were other people lining up to board my flight, lots of people crowding in on *my* plane. This was not right! *"I am a tired, special person who should not have to deal with people right now,"* I said to my humble, unselfish self.

Being a Medallion flyer, I raced to the front of the pack and charged through the gate ahead of the greedy mob. I hurried to the back of the great, sleeping aircraft, found my exit row (for extra leg room) window seat, grabbed two pillows from the overhead compartment, and settled in for a blissful snooze.

Not to happen. I couldn't believe it. Where were all these noisy people coming from? Didn't they know I needed rest? What really got me was someone was actually moving in on my middle seat, the one next to me, where I was going to turn and put my knees.

He was a very tall, dark-skinned man wearing a fashionable three-piece suit. He looked as if he might be from India or another eastern country. I pretended not to notice he was with a woman, his wife, who was dressed in her native attire, complete with nose rings and full-length garment. Because of the full-seating situation, she had to sit in the middle seat directly in front of her husband. Again, I pretended not to notice this. I didn't want to give up my window seat so she could sit next to her spouse. I was tired, after all, and hadn't heard her complain. I turned toward my little window, jammed my pillows into the crack, took a fatigued breath of stale, Delta air, and shut my poor, weary eyes.

I couldn't sleep. Try as I did, I just couldn't sleep. We were in the air nearly half an hour before I finally conceded and brought my seat into "its full and upright position" somewhere over Lake Ontario. I was exasperated; but if you can't sleep, you might as well eat, and the breakfast cart was coming down the aisle.

It's amazing how you can sit next to and rub shoulders with someone for most of an hour and not say anything. Being a good Christian, I eventually decided to say hello, and before too long, I found myself being cordial with this man. I asked him where he was from.

"From Pakistan," he answered. "My wife and I are here in America on a business trip," he said, nodding toward the seat in front of him.

"Oh, your wife," I said. "Hmmm. What kind of business are you in?" I added quickly.

"I am a dentist. My wife is an orthodontist. We have started, and now oversee, six clinics throughout our country. We were educated in America for the purpose of going back home and working with our people. Once a year we return to the United States to attend field seminars so we can keep up with the latest procedures and technology."

I was impressed with this man's spirit. He seemed to be very caring; a strong but gentle man.

"Do you mind my asking you ... your beliefs? Are you Muslim?" I asked. I trusted that this man's familiarity with Americans would allow me the grace to be a little more personal.

"Yes," he countered politely. "My mother, however, is a Caucasian from Austria (this may have explained the man's unusual height) and is of Christian heritage. She married my father, a Pakistani, who is, of course, Muslim. As a boy, I often conversed with my mother about Christianity, but ... I am a Muslim," he said. It seemed to me he was a little embarrassed to say so.

"Would you mind sharing with me about your faith? I would sincerely like to know what it is you believe."

For about a half an hour, the distinguished gentleman next to me shared the fundamentals of his religion. In closure, he divulged his deep concern over the hypocrisy he had witnessed among some in the faith who were very close to him. His last words, posed in the form of a question, were the ones that made me realize my purpose on that sleepless flight: "What I don't understand is, if God is supposed to be so loving, why do so many innocent people suffer?"

My heart skipped a beat. Not only was the issue of the "suffering innocent" one of my favorite teaching topics, but I was developing a genuine love for this sincere individual. It was an honor to sit and listen to him, and it was becoming clear to me that our encounter on the plane was no accident. Here was *one* of the Father's precious billions of children — a Muslim from the other side of the world — whom he longed to hold and heal.

"Do you mind if I share my beliefs and feelings about God?" I ventured.

"No, not at all, please do."

For the balance of our flight, I shared at length about the great and intense love of the Father and his passionate motivation for sending his Son, Jesus Christ, and how Jesus, in turn, fulfilled his role as the ultimate sacrifice on behalf of all people. I explained how Jesus provided us with the opportunity to be restored to our original place of security and significance as the Father's sons and daughters.

As I spoke, the man moved to the edge of his seat, closer to me. I could see he was fighting back tears. In the end, I told my new friend how the Father is the best father imaginable; how much he values *all* the people of the earth and grieves over *all* who suffer.

"He loves *you*, *so* much," I concluded.

The man was at first silent and aghast. Then he said, "I could never have imagined there could be such a God as this. Would you, perhaps, someday come to my country and share about this Father to my friends?"

Now I was aghast. "Yes, if it is in the Father's plan for me, it would be a great honor for me to come to your country; but you must know, he will *always* be beside you whenever you call out to him."

As he pulled his business card and address from his wallet, the plane touched down on the Minneapolis/St. Paul runway and carried us to our arrival gate. We were each to take other connecting flights from here, so we stood to our feet and made ready to leave. While I was reaching into the overhead compartment to retrieve my brief case and coat, I felt someone take hold of my arm. To my surprise, when I looked down, I was staring into the deep brown, moist eyes of the man's beautiful wife. She stared intently into my eyes and said: "I heard every word you shared with my husband. I thank you for all you said. I will never forget the words you have spoken."

I could barely respond.

When we reached the terminal and parted ways, the two travelers from Pakistan gave me smiles I will never forget. I stood still for a minute and prayed for them both as they walked from my view.

They were worth no sleep. They were worth *so* much more.

Chapter 24

The Second Highest Law and a Downtown Bar

"Teacher, which is the greatest commandment in the Law?"
Jesus replied: "'Love the Lord your God with all your heart
and with all your soul and with all your mind.' This is the
first and greatest commandment. And the second is like it:
'Love your neighbor as yourself.' All the Law and the
Prophets hang on these two commandments."
— Matthew 22:36-40

L ove your neighbor as yourself.

Loving someone else can't happen if you don't have a healthy love for yourself. And a healthy love for yourself can only come from the Father. It's his love that brings us a true sense of significance. Without it, it's almost impossible to make someone else feel loved and significant.

Christians who attempt evangelism, for example, will be improperly motivated if the issue of significance is not first resolved in their own life. The reason is simple. If they feel they've been cheated out of a sense of worth, then they'll make a subconscious determination that it's not fair for anyone else to experience a sense of worth. Thus, their evangelism won't be loving. They may come across as judgmental (an attitude not uncommon to the Church in general). These insecure folk will address those they perceive to be unlovely in the same way they perceive themselves — as unlovely.

So, enlisted among the ranks of Christianity's army are some insecure but well-meaning crusaders who feel they've done their spiritual duty when they've jumped in people's faces — in the name of the Lord, of course — having declared the truth irrespective of the outcome. It's tragic that, due to their own sense of low value, they place a greater value on the lesser laws than they do on the two primary laws: first, to love God with all their hearts, and then to love, with equal sincerity, those he created.

The good news is we have the answer for anyone who feels insecure and insignificant: the appropriation of the Spirit of sonship. Once we have a genuine encounter with the love of the Father and the inestimable worth he has placed upon us as his son or daughter, we are ready, rightly motivated, and empowered to carry his message of loving kindness to the people of this earth — *all* people, no matter what their beliefs, no matter what their situations.

———

It was early in the afternoon on a normal workday just two weeks before Christmas. I was working in my office in the Ministry Center when a good friend named John came knocking on my door.

Now, my friend John was what one might call an evangelist-type with somewhat of a prophetic side to him. It was this side that sometimes made me, the pastor-type, a little nervous. Oh, don't get me wrong, I really liked John — a lot. It was just that John often seemed to move in a more radical realm. His bold confidence tempted me to feel uneasy, sometimes guilty. I was never quite sure why. But whenever I saw John coming, I might do some quick, oh … soul searching, repenting … things like that.

"Hello, David!" John said with a brilliant smile. "I have a word from the Lord!"

"Ohhhhh (gulp) … good, John. That's good, John. Uh, what uh, is it … John?" I asked, wincing.

"Well, David, I believe the Lord wants us to do some singing and evangelism in all the bars in our city this Christmas."

"Ahhhh … well, you know, John, … let me tell you, John. Whenever anyone gets a word like you got, John, it's because God wants *him* … to obey that word. So God bless you, John, as you …" He cut me off.

"Wait a minute, David. The Bible teaches us that leaders are to lead by setting an example."

"It says that?" I replied, sheepish.

"Of course it does!" John shot back. "Don't you know that?"

"Of course I do … of course it does," I stuttered. "I knew … I knew that."

"Okay, then," John declared. "Let's go for it!"

I had to think of a way out of this. I had to think of a plan.

"Okay, John, I'll tell you what," I said, laughing to myself. "We could get our friends together, practice some Christmas songs, and go out to do a Christmas thing in the 'bars of our city' — only if you can get *all* the managers of these bars to say they would be happy to have us come into *their* bars and do *our* spiritual thing." *Ha! Great plan!*

John looked at me kind of strange, said, "Okay," and left my office. That look of his troubled me, but I shook it off and went back to my work.

About three hours later, just seconds before I was ready to leave for the day, John came bounding into my office like he had just won the lottery.

Uh oh, I thought to myself. *Bad plan.*

"David, you'll never guess what!"

"What? … John."

"All the bar managers in town said it would be just great for us to come to their bars and do our thing!"

"Are you sure, John?"

"Yep!"

"Did you explain to them what 'our thing' is, John?"

"Yep!"

"Great … John … wow."

I was thinking: *I hate you, John* (in a Christian way, of course).

So John got about twenty-five of our close church friends together, and we met for our first practice session before my not-so-much-anticipated "night out on the town." The practice went well. Much to my surprise, everyone seemed pretty up for the idea. I had written a couple of Christmas songs we drew on for the occasion. Plus, we added in several of the old standards with a little bit of spice for rendition's sake. We actually came up with a pretty decent program all in all.

The night came.

John had prearranged scheduled bar times for a full night of singing and … whatever. I still wasn't at all sure about this whole deal. But everyone met at the designated hour, and "the church" headed out for some good old everyday bar hopping. *I must be crazy*, I thought, *letting a prophet-type talk me into this.*

The first bar John had us "booked" into was the Outlaw Inn. *How appropriate*, I whined to myself. *John's gonna take us in there so we can all get shot. I'm liking this plan less and less every minute.*

We walked in the side door and stopped behind a wall that divided us from a band rocking out in the bar on the other side. There was one big party going on in there! I looked at John, hoping he would get another word from the Lord, like *leave*. He didn't.

After several minutes of guitars cranking, drums beating, and garbled sounds coming from the lead singer, the band noise stopped and the two hundred-plus lit-up partiers started whooping and hollering. After one last screech of feedback from the sound system, the band leader said, and I quote, "Well, we're gonna take a set break here for just a little while. There's gonna be some kind of church choir group that's gonna come in here and sing at y'all; but don't you worry, and don't go away, we'll be back real soon."

This time I almost said, *"I hate you, John,"* out loud. But it would have been all for naught. It was too late. I was the leader. I had to go in there.

We rounded the corner to face a mob of Outlaw party animals. They had their glasses in hand and their mouths open wide in total disbelief, as if to say in seasonal accord, "What in hell's blazes are *you* doin' here?"

And, of course, that's exactly what I was thinking. I felt like I was in the "Not OK Corral" with nothing but carols ... and no bullets. Really, though, it hit me. We had just walked into someone's "living room," if you will, without an invite.

To my surprise, however, the fear I had felt walking in disappeared. Instead, I began to feel a real sense of compassion for these "outlaws."

It dawned on me that it was an *honor* to be allowed to share a little bit of ourselves with these people. I looked around, and all I could think was how valuable they each were and how much the Father loved them. It was amazing to watch several of them join in with us on some of the old tunes. Most everyone seemed to be moved. I noticed a few folks fighting back tears.

Before I knew it, we had completed our last song, and I said a few departing words, concluding with something like this: "It's been an honor to spend a short while with you in this holiday season. Merry Christmas to you all, and may God truly bless you in the New Year." The people gave us a sincere and lengthy round of applause as we saluted them goodbye. "Merry Christmas," they shouted. *Father, be near them,* I prayed.

The rest of the evening went very well. It was all very memorable, but it was the last bar of the night I will remember most.

It was a small, cubbyhole of a bar squeezed inconspicuously into the middle of a block on the west side of Main Street. Funny that, in the countless trips I'd made up and down this street, I had never noticed it before.

The bar room itself was only eighteen or twenty feet wide. Long and narrow, it stretched unceremoniously from the front sidewalk to a quiet alley out back. Its timeworn walls and ceiling added to the ambience of solemn, smoky darkness. The red glow from an old jukebox against the back wall seemed to be the bar room's foremost yet feeble source of lighting; that and the small, hidden fluorescents positioned above the assorted bottles on the wall behind the bar.

There was no band. No party in this place. Barely any movement at all except from the bartender, who was drying and putting a glass away on a shelf above his head as we entered. About ten, maybe twelve people, mostly middle-aged and older, were seated randomly throughout the smoky, musty room. Two men sat at one of the small tables against the left wall. A man and a woman sat at another. Everyone else sat motionless and alone, a few by themselves at tables, the rest at the bar.

As the twenty-five of us pushed through the front door, everyone in the room turned their head and stared. These weren't stares of disbelief; these were stares of great uneasiness. *They* were the ones who were nervous. While the Outlaw Inn was like a living room, this place was like a bedroom. The gang and I were immediately sensitive to the reaction of the people here. It was easy to see these quiet, minding-their-own-business kind of folk viewed us outsiders as an uncomfortable intrusion and potential threat.

We said a few introductory words to break the ice and then began to sing. It was amazing to watch the atmosphere change as our music started to stir the darkness. A few joined in with us as best they could. An older woman at the far end of the bar mouthed a few words of an old, familiar melody, and then stopped to wipe her eyes. The presence of the Lord filled the bar room.

After saying a few more words and starting the last song, something happened I wasn't at all prepared for. The burly bartender shuffled down his side of the bar toward us. This lord of the bar had a huge barrel chest, which made the buttons on his short-sleeved shirt look as if they were holding on for dear life. His enormous, swollen belly buried his belt, and a distinct network of blue veins coursed across his red cheeks like river tributaries on a topical map. He had gray, thinning hair and a broad smile that exposed a set of crooked, tobacco-stained teeth.

He reached below the bar top, pulled out two magnums of champagne and twenty-five glasses, and began to pour.

Holy fruit cake! (or some such phrase) I gasped to myself. *Oh God, what am I going to do?* As I was freaking out, I tried to sing along with the group but was actually thinking: *Silent night, holy fright! I'm not calm; I'm not all right! I brought the wholecottonpickin' church with me and the man's serving booze!*

Now I was desperate. This was a major "between a rock and a hard place" deal here. What would my *Christian* friends think if I — their pastor — drank the champagne? And what would the barkeeper and his friends think if I didn't? *Oh God, pleeeeeze speak to me!*

Then, in my mind, I distinctly heard a deep, strong, authoritative voice say these words:

"Pick ... up ... the glass."

Is that really you, God?

"Yessss."

The song was over. I had already repeated it several times, and it was time to do something. The room was dead silent. The bartender leaned forward, palms down on the bar, and stared into my eyes, beaming from ear to ear. With a nervous and indecisive smile, I reached for ... the alcohol.

Trying to hide my jitters, I clenched and hesitantly lifted the glass — *and the whole choir zoomed for the champagne!* They charged the glasses like twenty-five calves after one cow at suppertime.

I was stunned. *I thought you were Christians!* I shouted speechlessly.

I looked at the old man behind the bar, who was as proud as a peacock and as happy as a lark. My heart — our hearts — went out to him with genuine compassion and gratitude. He had just given us an expensive gift from *his* heart — the gift of ... alcohol!

I lifted my bubbly drink higher, and all my friends joined me as we paused to salute and honor our kind host and his friends. Throughout the bar, glasses were raised. "We truly hope this will be a wonderful Christmas for you and that your New Year will be one of your best ever," I said. "May God be with you all!"

As we turned to leave, they gave us a cheer. "Merry Christmas," they said, "and a Happy New Year!"

When we got outside, Main Street was nearly empty except for a few parked cars belonging to late night patrons. We huddled close together on the sidewalk, circled around the base of a street lamp that illuminated the giant December snowflakes falling around us. Arms on each other's shoulders, we stood quietly, shoes deep in three inches of fresh, fluffy snow. We looked at each other for a long time without saying a word. It was a special moment. We had just been ... to church.

It's time to commit ourselves as caregivers and dedicate our lives to observing the second highest law — right after the first and well before the rest. It's time to love all the other children in the earth.

Chapter 25

Letting Go

*"I prayed for this child, and the Lord has granted me what I
asked of him. So now I give him to the Lord."*
—1 Samuel 1:27-28

———

*T*he objective in all our caregiving is to see our children become healthy sons and daughters of the Father. And then, one day, we release them to become caregivers themselves, joining the Father in his cause for the care of others.

I always knew the time would come when Kathy and I would have to let our children go. I'll be the first to confess letting go isn't always easy. Our first experience with this came much sooner than we expected.

It was during late winter of 1984. We had invited our good friend, Gary Stevens, over for an evening meal. At the time, he was serving as the director of a Youth With A Mission base in Hong Kong. He had traveled to Montana to visit his parents and would be speaking in our church in the morning following his visit with us. Gary had a somewhat notorious reputation as a master recruiter for missions. With plenty of vision and a million-dollar smile, he had the ability to swoop up almost anyone he wanted for any number of his short- or long-term mission campaigns. Those who knew him well referred to him affectionately as "the Asian vacuum cleaner."

Following a pleasant time around the table with Gary and our whole family, I said, "Gary, why don't you go into the living room and make yourself comfortable. Kathy and I will deal with these dishes, and then we'll come in and join you." So Gary got up, Kathy started the dishwater, and I began to clear the table.

During my third trip from the table to the sink, I paused, dishes in hand, to notice that Gary-the-vacuum-cleaner was sitting on the sofa talking in an eager and suspicious manner with *my* Kimberly.

What?! No way! I thought, hoping what was happening was not happening. *She's only thirteen years old. Not even Gary would try to recruit a thirteen-year-old girl into missions. Nah.* Still, I continued to pause on every trip between table and sink, my eyebrows furrowed as I scrutinized the scene. With the table finally cleared, I forced the matter out of my mind, grabbed a towel, and began to dry dishes. After drying only one lousy dish, Kimberly came running into the kitchen with "shouts of acclamation."

"Daddy! Daddy! You'll never guess what! Gary has invited me to come to Asia for the summer to join a Summer of Service missions team in Hong Kong! Isn't this wonderful, Daddy? You always told me to go for it! Isn't this wonderful?!"

I jerked my head sharply to glare at Gary, who was trying to fake reading a magazine while, at the same time, smiling a cunning smile, his sly tongue in his cheek. *I hate you, Gary,* I said to myself (in a Christian way).

Kimi continued standing in front of me, innocent and quiet; patiently waiting for my endorsement. I wasn't letting her go to Asia. I had to think of a plan.

In no time it came to me and it involved Michelle. I didn't *think* Michelle would respond at all like her sister, Kimberly. She was two years older and would certainly not want to spend her entire summer on the other side of the world. My plan was simple. I said, "Kimi, honey, you can go to Asia — but only if your sister would be willing to go and spend the *whole* summer in Asia with you." *Ha!*

Kimi studied my face for a moment, said, "Okay," turned, and trotted confidently out of the kitchen. I stood there motionless and a little confused as I watched her leave; then I shook the whole incident off and went back to drying dishes. Before I could finish the next plate, Michelle and Kimberly both came bounding around the corner.

"Oh, thank you, Daddy, thank you!" Michelle said. "I can't believe it! Thank you for letting Kimi and me go to Asia! Thank you, thank you!"

"Michelle?!" Astonished, I stared down at her in total disbelief. "Is that you, Michelle? Michelle, sweetheart, what are you thinking? You don't want to spend the whole summer in Asia! Do you know where Hong Kong is, Michelle? Go get the world globe out of your room."

The girls ran off to their room. Before I could close my gaping mouth, they were back, globe in hand.

"Now, Michelle, show me where we live on this globe." She smiled and pointed at Montana. "Uh huh, and now show me where Hong Kong is," I said smugly. After spinning the globe a few times, she smiled again and pointed to the city of Hong Kong. "Now, Michelle, honey, do you notice that big *blue* thing between Montana and Hong Kong?"

"Uh huh."

"That is called an ocean. It's a *big* ocean."

"Uh huh."

"Well?"

"It doesn't look that big to me."

I guess we needed a bigger globe. At any rate, I wasn't letting my girls go to Asia. I had to think of a plan. Again, it came to me in no time.

"Now girls, you both know your mom and I would just *love* for you both to be able to go." With a look of cynicism, Kathy glared at me, waiting for the revelation of my next remarkable plan. "But *unfortunately*, girls, we just don't have the money to send you. You'd have to somehow get all the money yourselves. Perhaps we'll be able to send you on a trip like this when you're older. We're sorry, girls, we're *very* sorry."

But I forgot to figure in Grandpa. Not only did grandpas, grandmas, and every other relative get involved, but most of our so-called friends did too. At church the next day, every one began giving the girls money. It was brutal. The girls had all the money needed for the entire trip by about four o'clock the next afternoon. I was stunned. I had no more plans.

After all was said and done — and Gary-the-vacuum-cleaner had fled the state — Kathy and I came to the conclusion it must be the will of God. So the girls made preparations for their great adventure. There was a lot to do to get them ready, but they had plenty of time to do it in. In fact, they were all set and ready to go nearly two full months before their departure date. It was during those last two months I noticed the girl's excitement over the trip seemed to taper off a bit. I didn't give it much concern.

Finally, the big day arrived. Kathy and I and the girls packed up the car and headed off on the four-and-a-half-hour drive to Spokane, Washington, where we had found the least expensive round-trip airfare to the Orient. About midway, I began noticing something a little different about this road trip. Normally, there would be a mix of singing and chattering as we drove; the girls would start a song, and the rest of us would join right in. But no one was singing this morning. I decided to try starting a song, but for some reason, I just couldn't think of one.

After an extended period of solemn quietness, Kimi broke the silence. She leaned forward, put her chin on the backrest of the front seat and said, "Daddy? Mom?"

"Yes, honey," I replied.

"Do you think our grandparents and relatives and any other people who sponsored us would be disappointed with us if we came home, say … a week earlier than we had planned?"

"No, honey, I don't think so …"

I barely finished my sentence and Kimi popped in again, "Daddy, what if we wanted to come home two or three weeks earlier?"

Kathy and I looked at each other, and then Kathy looked out her window. I was beginning to interpret our silent ride "Uh … girls, Mom and I want you to know you can come home whenever you want to, but we think it's best if you try keeping your original plans. But later, if you need to come home early, you can. Okay?"

"Okay, Daddy," they both mumbled, sliding back against their seats. In the rear view mirror, I could see they, too, were now each staring out their own windows, fighting their growing insecurity without success. Pensive, I drove on, staring at the unfriendly highway ahead.

In far too little time, we arrived at the Spokane airport. I yanked a parking ticket from the gate, pulled into a three-tiered parking complex, and parked our car facing the airport facilities across the street. After turning off the engine, I just sat there for some time, my right hand holding onto the car keys that were still hanging in their ignition position. Glaring at the buildings in front of us, I thought to myself, *Why do they call it a terminal? Why not … airplane station?*

"Honey," Kathy said with a high, wake-up-dear-husband voice. "Are we going to get out of the car?"

"Yes," I responded, returning to reality. "Yes, let's get out of the car." My arms and legs felt heavy, sluggish, uncooperative. Still, I somehow managed to pull the keys from the ignition, push open my door, and extract myself from the vehicle. I trekked slowly to the rear of the car and popped open the trunk. There they were; my daughters' suitcases — *massive* numbers of suitcases.

I used to lift diaper bags and play pens out of a trunk similar to this, I thought. I began to lift the luggage, piece by piece, until it was all standing upright behind me on the blacktop. I slammed the trunk shut, and with suitcases in hand, we all trudged solemnly across the street to the *terminal.*

After checking the girls in at the front counter and then finding their departure gate, we still had about forty-five minutes before take-off. We took all that time to go over last minute details.

"Michelle, honey, until you arrive in Hong Kong, I want you to keep your watch set on Montana time. Kimberly, I want you to keep setting your watch according to the time zones, okay? Now, we want you to call us as soon as you arrive. That should be in eighteen hours. We want you to call us in eighteen hours *exactly.* Do you both understand that? Eighteen hours *exactly.*"

Somehow, our forty-five minutes took only four or five, and the announcement came over the loud speaker that it was time for the girls to board. Now, being the unselfish person I am, I suggested to the girls that we allow all the other passengers to board first … you know, show the others honor by being last to board?

I hugged Michelle, and Kathy hugged Kimberly. Then I hugged Kimberly, and Kathy hugged Michelle. Then I hugged Michelle, and Kathy hugged Kimberly. Then I hugged Kimberly, and …

After what seemed like hardly any time at all, the stewardess at the boarding gate seemed to get annoyed with my unselfishness and said, "Sir, the captain would like to *leave* now."

"Okay, okay," I responded, and we hugged our daughters two last times. Then they turned, holding each other's hands, and walked slowly toward the tunnel, which led down to the abyss. As they started to enter the aircraft, they looked back one more time. I'll never forget the look on their faces. It was as if they were crying out for us to save them. It took all my spiritual strength, plus Kathy pulling on the back of my shirt, to keep me from going after them. I almost did, except they suddenly turned and disappeared.

It helps to go over to the window and put your nose and hands on the glass. From there, we watched the cold, giant metal bird pull away from us with our daughters inside. In only moments, it rumbled down the runway and roared out of our sight into the western skies. We kept on watching, hoping to see one last little shine off its ominous silver wings. Kathy and I turned to each other. I was fighting tears; Kathy had given up fighting them. We held hands as we walked through the terminal and out to our car. The long ride home held no singing either. We learned months later that as we were driving home and the girls were flying farther and farther away, Michelle continued to speak words of comfort to her weepy younger sister.

At one point, I heard Kathy — a loving and dedicated caregiver — verbally affirm her willingness to "let go" by paraphrasing words spoken thousands of years before to Esther of the Old Testament: "They must have been created for such a time as this."

———

Eighteen hours later, we were both by the phone. Twenty hours later, we were both by the phone. Twenty-four, twenty-six, twenty-eight hours later … we were still by the phone. Suddenly, Kathy said, "What if the slave traders have them? They could be hanging over the backs of llamas right now, going through the mountains of Tibet, scared, starving …"

"Honey! Stop that! That could never happen — I don't think."

Finally, the phone rang. Kathy and I each jumped to the extensions. After some strange phone noise, we heard, "Dad? Mom?"

"Yes! Michelle, is that you?"

"Yes-yess," returned a distant, broken, and sorrowful little voice.

"What's the matter, Michelle? Honey, are you okay?"

"I ... don't ... know!"

"What?! What do you mean, you don't know? Michelle! What's wrong?!"

"Maybe you should talk to Kimberly."

"What?! Kimberly! Is that you, sweetheart?"

"Yes-yess," returned another distant, but even more broken and sorrowful little voice.

"Kimi! What's wrong with Michelle?"

"She's ... curryyying!"

"Crying? Why is she crying? Kimi, what's wrong?!"

"Well, we waited at the airport in Hong Kong for eight hours, and the YWAM people didn't come and pick us up!" *I HATE THE VACUMM CLEANER!* I raged to myself — almost in a Christian way.

"And Daddy ... no one speaks English here, and we couldn't find the number to the YWAM base, and we tried to call for help from an operator, but the operator couldn't understand us, and finally, about midnight, a tall young man said, 'Are you Michelle and Kimberly?', and we went with him to the YWAM base, and then it was so late the phones didn't work, and we had to try and sleep on Gary's office floor, but then these people came in and woke us up this morning, and our hair doesn't work because it is sooo humid, and we're *really* saaad!!"

"Kimi, sweetheart, everything's going to be okay now, I promise." I blurted out some Scripture verse that didn't even comfort me at the time, and we continued trying to encourage them the best way we knew how. We told them to call us in one week, at the latest, to let us know how things were going. We eventually had to say an excruciating goodbye.

The girls told us later that as soon as they hung up, a wonderful YWAM staff girl, having seen their distress, gave them each a big hug and welcome. She pointed them to a hot shower, later gave them a delicious breakfast, introduced them to their Summer of Service team members, and the girls then began the most wonderful summer of their entire lives.

And we knew nothing for one full week!

There they were on the other side of the world. In a strange new place, outside the safety of their own home, our children would learn an advanced lesson in trust — and caregiving. There, they would discover more about their significance as their heavenly Father's daughters, more about their well-being, and a huge lesson about purpose.

But back home, my significance was marginal; my well-being was toast, and my purpose? Shoot Gary.

It's hard letting go.

Chapter 26

The Reward

*All the ends of the earth will remember and turn to the Lord,
and all the families of the nations will bow down before him.*
— Psalm 22:27

———

*T*he streets of the area known as New Territories are not always friendly. Tourists to Hong Kong normally don't traffic this part of the city, but it is here a great density of hurting and needy people can be found. YWAM Hong Kong sent one of its small teams of recruits into this area for a summer of special ministry and service. Michelle and Kimberly were two of only a few Westerners on this team.

One of the ministry activities of the girls' team was to put on street dramas followed by brief evangelistic messages or testimonies. Afterward, the team followed up with one-on-one witnessing and sharing. This type of outreach presentation was common in YWAM's ministry around the world and had already proven to be very successful. New Territories was no exception.

While doing these presentations and other activities, the YWAM leaders couldn't help but notice a group of teenage boys, dressed similarly, who shadowed the team wherever they went in the city. Even during the team's recreation times, these boys were nearby, sitting on a wall or standing in an alley, always watching every move the team made. The team leaders were told by other locals that these boys were members of a major Hong Kong gang known as the Triads. Concerned for the team's safety, the leaders asked all the team members to travel in groups of at least two when outside the YWAM center.

One day, Kimberly, the youngest on the team, and an older teenage friend, Kelly, decided to take a walk from the center to a local courtyard a short distance away. When the two girls got there, they paused to sit down on a concrete bench.

Some minutes later, a large Chinese man, reeking of alcohol, staggered toward the girls. Without warning, he grabbed both of them and began aggressively pawing them all over. The girls both screamed and wrestled to get free. The man began to focus his efforts on Kelly. Kimberly pulled at the man in an effort to get him off of her friend. Kelly squirmed loose and ran off frantically in the direction of the YWAM center. The man then turned and grabbed Kimberly again.

By the way, Kimberly told us this story as I was driving us all home from Spokane on the girl's return trip.

"*What?!* He did *what?* What happened? What happened next, honey?" I bellowed, almost driving off the highway imagining Kimberly in this frightening situation.

"Daddy, he kept grabbing me in places. I screamed and fought, and I finally got loose and hit him in the face with my fist!"

"Good! Then what, honey? Then what?"

"I ran, but he chased me!"

"What?! Did you get away!?"

"He was so much bigger and faster than me. I ran as fast as I could, but he was catching up to me."

"Yes, yes! And then?"

"Then the most incredible thing happened!"

"Yes?!"

"Dad, Mom … God spoke to me! And he said, 'Kimberly, stop and turn around.' So I did. I stopped and spun around to face the man chasing me."

"Go on! Go on!"

"I couldn't believe it! This man who was running after me came to a dead stop right in front of me, looked up above my head, opened his mouth in complete horror, and raced off like a crazy man in the opposite direction!"

(Just what did the man see standing behind Kimberly?!)

"Daddy, I turned around. I couldn't see anyone … but I know it was … an angel! Really — an angel!"

(Can you imagine this? Right behind Kimberly, with his hands on her shoulders, fire *blasting* from his mouth — THE GODZILLA ANGEL!!)

"Mom, Dad; it was amazing, absolutely amazing!"

Thank you, Father! Thank you!

"I ran as fast as I could, caught up with Kelly, and we both raced to the center. When we got there, everyone huddled around us as we shared the story. We had a meeting … we prayed … we thanked the Father for protecting us. We made a new rule: From then on, we would only go out in groups of six!"

Kimi then told us that about an hour or so after the meeting there was a knock at the door of the center. Standing on the front porch was about a half dozen or more of the Triad gang members! The YWAM leader moved quickly to the door. Through the interpreter, gang members said, "We want to see the young blonde girl."

The YWAM leader said, "I'm sorry. The young blonde girl is not available any more today." Kimi, however, ducked her head under her leader's arm and stood on the front step, facing the boys. Her leader pulled her close, and the two of them, plus an interpreter, faced the gang.

The gang leader looked at Kimberly and said, "We heard about what happened to you today in the park. We are *very* mad. That man who attacked you will *never* bother you again. My friends and I are going to *protect* you and all your friends the whole time you are in New Territories."

A few days later, that same gang leader — and his friends — dedicated their lives to Christ and became sons of the Father!

Who was protecting whom?

———

Apparently, a day off was a rare treat for the busy Summer of Service team in the New Territories. Every day had been packed with new challenges and rewarding results. (Upon their return from Hong Kong, Kathy and I would see pictures of our two daughters standing in the middle of large groups of Asian teenagers; just some of the many kids Michelle and Kimberly helped lead to Christ and the Father all during that memorable summer.) Once in a great while, the girls and their team mates got to take a day off for rest and relaxation.

On one such day, Michelle, Kimberly, and a few of the others were heading across the city to do some shopping. As they walked down the sidewalk, they came upon an old homeless woman sitting on a pile of her belongings, which she had shoved up against a building. The kids could see she was blind. Her eyes were glazed and milky-white. In front of her was a small bucket with a few coins in it. In her hands, which rested on her lap, she held a harmonica. She sat without emotion, staring into her dark and lonesome world, passively listening for the sounds of new foot traffic and potential generosity.

As the kids passed her by, one of them said, "Don't you think we should go back and help her somehow?"

"It's our day off," the others said in unanimous reply.

They kept on walking a short way farther. Then, they all came to a stop together, turned, and walked back to where the homeless woman was sitting.

They knelt down beside her; each dropping a few coins in her bucket. Then, through the interpreter, they asked if she was hungry. She nodded her head yes, so the kids bought food for her from a street vendor only yards away. The girls were surprised at how greedily the woman ate. "She ate enough for three or four people," Michelle said. "We kept bringing food ... she kept on eating!"

Finally, she seemed to have her fill, and the kids continued to talk with her. A small crowd of locals began to gather around the team.

"Have you ever heard of Jesus?" one of the kids asked the woman.

"Yes," the old woman said in sudden anger. "I heard of him from a missionary when I was a child. Jesus made me blind."

Hesitating, the kids looked at each other and then asked if they could pray for her. Caught off guard, the woman didn't know quite how to respond. The kids took that as a go ahead and began to pray. As each took turns praying, they could hear the growing crowd around them begin to murmur.

A prayer went up something like this: "Dear Father, show this woman you love her. Touch her ... heal her of her hurts ... heal her, Father."

As the prayers continued, the old woman seemed annoyed, and the crowd got louder. The team began to feel uneasy as the woman blurted out some words in her native language. All at once, she shouted and stood to her feet. The crowd noise intensified. Michelle and Kimberly and some of the team began backing away in an effort to leave.

"Wait! Wait!" the interpreter cried. "You don't understand! The woman is saying '*I can see!*'"

Another birthright delivered — on a day off in Hong Kong.

Chapter 27

It's Your Time!

But when the time had fully come, God sent his Son ...
that we might receive the full rights of sons.
— Galatians 4:4-5

⁓

Many summers have gone by since the girls' amazing experience across the Pacific. I remember as if it were yesterday how wonderful it was to have them back home and in our care.

What an incredible gift these four children have been. Being their dad and loving them as much as I do have been huge keys to unlocking a clear understanding of the Father's love for me and all of his children.

Thank you, Father, for my children.

Most importantly, thank you for your phenomenal, driving love that's made it possible for each of us to become one of *your* children.

⁓

Dear Reader,

  If you haven't already taken the step, today could be your day for a "great transition." This could be your time to move from an unhealthy self-perception to an honorable one. You can choose to move from a weak and vulnerable state to a much more secure one; from a less-than-fulfilling way of life to a much more meaningful one.

  If these are the things you've always wanted; if you know there is an issue in your life that needs to be "fixed," then I encourage you to simply have, in your own way, a sincere conversation with your Father. Tell him you need him. Ask him to help you. He will.

  I urge you to make the choice. Step out of your past, choose to be changed in your present, and get on into your future as a son or daughter of the King.

  The following list is a summary of all that's been said. It's not all-inclusive, but it contains what I believe are principles for living in the Spirit of sonship. If you're hearing the confirming voice of the Spirit, then plant these principles deep inside and make them your own for as long as you live. That would be forever.

· Leave your unhealthy memories behind; speak forgiveness to those who have hurt you.

· Ask forgiveness from your Father for making choices independently from him.

· Begin or renew your shared relationship with him; feel the embrace of your ultimate Caregiver.

· Receive and take possession of your birthright; it came by way of the Captain.

· Believe and declare that you are one of the Father's significant sons or daughters.

· Keep speaking to your soul; take daily command over your feelings and emotions.

· Be at peace, grow, and flourish in your new and wonderful state of well-being.

· Live as one of the King's royal soldiers; be a strong, loving caregiver to others.

And here is my sincerest prayer for you: I'm asking the Father to do something new and powerful in your life. I'm asking him to give you a revelation of your birthright — the one in your hand — and to fill you with the Spirit of sonship. Finally, I'm asking that he send his Spirit to spend time with you, leading you into a deep understanding of your new significance, well-being, and purpose. That's what I'm praying for. That's what I believe for. Let it be, Father. It's *this one's* time.

———

Having heard some of my stories, would you join me in creating a new one? We can start right now. Open your spirit's eyes and envision this with me:

You and I are sitting together with our family — the King's family — in the royal dining hall of the King's palace. The majestic room, full of warmth and color, hums with the excitement of good fellowship. While we share in a spectacular feast set before us, we reflect on all the things that have brought us to this amazing place of restored significance. Though it goes unspoken, we both recognize a common sense of honor, peace, and meaning neither of us had known in any other time of our lives.

But now, it's time. Our Father and his eldest Son, both seated at the head of the table, push back their chairs and stand to their feet. Understanding there is a mission, we all rise together and get ready to go. All eyes are on the Son, the Captain, as he makes his way toward the dining hall's massive doors. Without hesitation, we follow him through the great hallway and down the many steps to the vast courtyard below.

Angels lead our noble steeds from the stables out back. All of us — brothers and sisters — mount up on white horses for the mission at hand; soldiers of the King.

As the last of the soldiers take hold of their reins, a sudden silence falls. The Father takes his place on the highest courtyard step. As he surveys his army with loving admiration, a loud voice from among us declares: "Father! It's an honor to serve you. We're honored to go on your behalf! No matter where you send us; no matter what it takes, it will always be our privilege to ride for you and the sake of your children!"

"For you, Father, and the sake of your children!" rises the unison cry.

The thunderous chanting suddenly drops to a hush as our Father gestures to speak.

"I love each of you so much. I'm very proud of you. Remember, don't ever be afraid. Trust in your Captain. He will always be with you, and I … will always be with you. This is my promise. You are my sons and daughters!

Then the Captain shouts: "Open up the gates!"

It's time … it's *your* time. Let's ride.

Epilogue: Full Circle

O n a summer day in 1972, ten years before my life-changing encounters with the Father and while serving as a high school pastor of a church in Anaheim, California, I received an amazing promise. It happened on a Monday as I was walking alone across the huge, circular auditorium of what was then known as Melodyland Christian Center. Heading up one of the many church aisles, I saw a man, the only other person in the building, walking toward the large glass doors that led to an outdoor courtyard.

When I reached the top of the aisle and turned to go out the same doors, I could see him standing outside, silhouetted against the bright midmorning sunlight. Then he made a quick turnaround, walked back inside, and stopped in front of the doors, looking at me. I realized, to my surprise, that it was the guest speaker who had spoken in the previous night's service.

His name was Dick Mills, a man with a powerful, prophetic ministry. After delivering stirring messages, he would often invite people to come to the platform and meet him briefly. There, he would offer each person a specific Scripture he felt prompted to give. The responses were always something to watch. It was easy to see by the reactions of those he met that the verses he shared with them were most meaningful.

Though I had watched him from a distance on several occasions, I had never met him before. And now, there he was, standing in front of me. He was a tall, strong man. As I slowed and stopped in front of him, looking at his kind and confident face, he smiled. He reached out to me, put his hand on my shoulder, and spoke these words: "Young man, the Lord wants you to know something; this is his promise to you. It's Isaiah 59:21." This is what he said:

> "As for me, this is my covenant with them," says the Lord. "My Spirit, who is on you, and my words that I have put in your mouth will not depart from your mouth, or from the mouths of your children, or from the mouths of their descendants from this time on and forever," says the Lord.

I've never forgotten that promise.

And now, it has been a long time since the days of track meets, pageants, palm-tree pony tails, and socks. Since then, Michelle, Kimberly, Jeffrey, and Michael have become outstanding adults and exceptional caregivers. They have given us twelve very special grandchildren. Along the way, each of our children has ventured out on other mission trips to various parts of the world. Michael worked one summer helping a church in Mexico. Jeff spent nearly a year working in around fifteen countries throughout Europe, some of that time organizing a number of Christian youth camps in Russia. Michelle worked in the Philippines and Australia, then went back one more time to the New Territories in Hong Kong.

In 2004, Kimberly ventured out on the trip of her lifetime. Kathy and I hadn't known that while she was in Hong Kong with her sister twenty-two years earlier, God had planted a seed in her heart. In August, Kimberly and her husband, Jason, flew to the Orient for a most important mission. They returned home to Montana having rescued a beautiful little ten-month-old girl, who, as a newborn, had been left in a basket on the steps of a building in Jiujang City in the province of Jiangxi in central eastern China. Her name is Lily Michelle

Ya Lin Bridwell. She is our granddaughter; she is a princess; she is a daughter of the King.

From abandonment to belonging, from unclaimed to claimed, she now rides among the riders, her own birthright in hand. And one day, I believe you will see her charging forward through the desert on her own white horse, her dark eyes focused, black hair flowing.

About the Author

David Graham is a former pastor, businessman, and the founding director of Youth With A Mission (YWAM) Montana. For many years, in churches across North America, David has taught a healing message about the ultimate Parent — Father God — and his honored sons and daughters. David is also the author of a number of songs including "In Moments Like These," which is still sung in many different languages around the world.

David and his wife, Kathy, live close by their kids and grand-kids in the Flathead Valley of Northwest Montana.

www.theyridewhitehorses.com